Outwitting Bears

Living in Bear Country

Gary Brown

The Lyons Press

For Pat, Kris, and Janine,
who have outwitted and eluded bears,
as well as bison and elk, during the many years
at our medley of homes in bear country

Printed in Canada

Designed by Compset, Inc.

10 9 8 7 6 5 4 3 2 1

Library of Congress Cataloging-in-Publication Data is available on file.

Acknowledgments

This book was written with the enormous assistance of many individuals and organizations across the North American continent, from Texas to Georgia, from California to Churchill, Manitoba, and to Alaska's Kodiak Island and North Slope.

I greatly appreciate the help of each of the many persons that spent their valuable time, not always with their supervisor's support, providing me with information, ideas, and anecdotes of their specific geographic area.

A special thank you to: Bonnie Reynolds McKinney, Wildlife Technician, Texas Parks and Wildlife; David Carlock, Senior Wildlife Biologist, Georgia Department of Natural Resources; Cathy Shroshire, Heritage Program Coordinator of the Mississippi Department of Wildlife, Fisheries and Parks; Paul Davidson, Executive Director of the Black Bear Conservation Committee in Louisiana (Lower Mississippi Valley); Mark Haroldson, Interagency Grizzly Bear Study Team, Bozeman, Montana; Kate McCurdy, Wildlife

Biologist, Black Bear Management Program, Yosemite National Park; Johnny Johnson, Johnny Johnson Photography, Anchorage; Ron Barnett, beekeeper, Belgrade, Montana; James Cardoza, Wildlife Biologist, Massachusetts Division of Fisheries and Wildlife; Harry Reynolds III, Alaska Department of Fish and Game; Craig George and Geoff Carroll, Alaska north slope group; Kevin Frey, Grizzly Bear Management Specialist, State of Montana; Dave Wedum, Choteau, Montana, retired game warden, and state lion/bear trapper; Paul Schullery, author and historian, for your assistance, support and encouragement; and Lilly Golden, Editor at Large, The Lyons Press, for the assistance and especially your patience.

Contents

Introduction

"Bears are neither 'good' nor 'bad.' They simply are. They are bears."
—Jack Samson, 1979, outdoor author, former editor of *Field & Stream*

Nearly everyone is familiar with a bear of some type: the clever black bears of North America; the mysterious polar bears of the Arctic; the huge brown bears found on some Alaskan islands (Kodiak bears) and the Kamchatka Peninsula of Russia; the grizzlies (brown bears) of the United States, Canada, Europe, and Asia; the intriguing, and extremely endangered, giant pandas of China; the unusual sloth bears of India and south-central Asia; the Asiatic black bears of southeast and south-central Asia; South America's only species, the spectacled bears; and the smallest of all, the sun bears of Indonesia and southeast Asia.

There has for millennia been a guarded coexistence between bears and people, but their relationship has not always been one of total conflict. Marvelous wild animals, bears have long been extremely meaningful ingredients in people's lives. Mythical, sometimes holy, exhilarating, intriguing, and humanlike, they have provided subsistence, sport, excitement, comfort, and utilitarian and spiritual values.

Humans have lived in bear country for thousands of years, but today more people than ever are changing their lifestyles, seeking rural living, seclusion, or mountain retreats, and they are moving into the realm of the bears. People, too, need wilderness and space. According to Aldo Leopold, in *A Sand County Almanac,* "Wilderness is the raw material out of which man has hammered the artifact called civilization."

"Bear country" is anywhere these large animals normally reside and find the necessities of survival as individuals and species. Bears also require wildness—undisturbed expanses without human presence and intervention. The requirements of humans and bears are not exactly the same, but they have many similarities. According to David Rockwell, in *Giving Voice To Bear,* ". . . the Yavapai of Arizona said, 'Bears are like people except that they can't make fire. . . .' "

For as long as humans and bears have lived together, the former have applied their images, perceptions, beliefs, and feelings to bears. And just possibly, the bears have thought to themselves that those two-legged things act just like bears. John Muir reflected on these similarities when he wrote, "Bears are made of the same dust as we, breathe the same winds and drink of the same waters. . . ."

This book is not just about bears, but humans as well; you and me. In fact, the focus is not equal, but weighted toward the lives, activities, and actions of the people "living" with the three species of these extraordinary mammals that exist in North America—the American black bears (*Ursus americanus*); the brown bears (*Ursus arctos*), including the sub-species grizzly bears (*Ursus arctos horribilis*) and Kodiak brown bear (*Ursus arctos middendorffi*); and the polar bears (*Ursus maritimus*). Throughout these pages, American black bears are referred to as *black bears. Brown bears* will include grizzly bears unless otherwise noted.

Outwitting Bears is written for all interested readers, but most specifically for persons living or planning to live where bears reside—in bear country. It is for those permanent or temporary residents who must prevent conflicts with these animals, protecting themselves and their property, and preserving the bears and their habitat. The book is about understanding bears, recognizing potential conflicts, and taking preventive measures to "outwit" them.

Now, what is "outwitting?" Various sources define "wit" as shrewdness or ingenuity, the power of reasoning, the quality of being alert and observant. "Outwitting" is characterized as getting the better of by superior ingenuity, cleverness or cunning; to outmaneuver, outthink, finesse; to fool. Bears can be outwitted, but doing so requires our finest efforts.

A resident of bear country has additional responsibilities, as well as risks. Living compatibly with bears—coexisting—is a challenging undertaking, though not as difficult as living with some human neighbors. Bears have a much different motivational source than people. They are driven and influenced not only by their brains, but by their stomachs as well. Outwitting bears is not only a battle of wits, but a contest of humans' wits and actions against the bears' very powerful and basic desire for food, as well as their deep curiosity and high intelligence. Other animals such as squirrels and deer may be readily outwitted, but bears, with their intelligence, are capable of reversing the role and outwitting us. The bottom line is that you are in a battle of intelligence.

The purpose of *Outwitting Bears* is to provide guidance in recognizing bear attractants and potential problems, and to provide the solutions that prevent conflicts. More specifically, outwitting bears prevents habituation and food conditioning of bears which results in property damage and, depending on human presence, possibly personal injury or even death—most commonly, the death of bears. Yes, outwitting bears saves them. Each of us has a responsibility to protect bears and other wildlife as we share their country. The challenges of living in bear country vary from area to area, and I have attempted to address the bear problems in all reaches of Canada and the United States.

A basic understanding of these symbols of wildness is an essential foundation for outwitting them. My objectives are to provide the knowledge and understanding to pre-

vent conflicts, and the information to manage serious encounters with bears, such as attacks.

As a resident of bear country, appreciate and enjoy the
fact that you live in a unique place. Respect the bears as
neighbors—coexist by outwitting them.

"Is that bear on your property or are you in his front yard?"
    —Idaho Department of Fish and Game

One

Bears—A Natural History

"... *the sequoia of the animals.* ..."
—John Muir, 1901

If you are to live in bear country and outwit bears, understanding them is a necessity. You need to know what they are capable of, why they behave as they do, and how they live their day-to-day lives in search of food.

Physical Description

Bears are the only large omnivores on the planet—meaning that in addition to being big, they generally eat anything and everything. They all have basically the same shape, with heavily constructed, strong, and durable bodies. Enormous strength and power is displayed by their excellent digging prowess, great speed and endurance, and the incredible ability to remove walls from buildings or, in the case of grizzly bears, to kill and carry away an adult elk. In *The Sacred Paw,* Paul Shepard and Barry Sanders write:

When a biologist once attempted to define the uniqueness of man as the only animal who could walk or run many miles, swim a river, and then climb a tree, he overlooked the bears, who can do all of these faster and with more endurance than man, not to mention digging a fifteen-foot-deep hole or killing a horse with a blow of the forepaws.

Generally, the heads of bears are huge in proportion to their bodies: long, wide across the forehead, with prominent eyebrow ridges, small eyes, and broad nostrils. Their teeth are large, set in jaws powered by massive muscles, and designed to bite, shear, hold, grind, and crush. The structure of bears' skulls and teeth is very much that of carnivores, though with omnivore modifications.

Bears' necks and legs are relatively short, with forelegs shorter than hind legs; they strike, handle, and dig with the powerful forefeet only. Their curved, strong claws are hard, and may be used to strike prey, rip and tear, rapidly dig a hole adequate in size to house a bear, break open house windows, hook and pull down vehicle doors, crush and open garbage containers, and tear off doors of buildings.

However, these impressive implements can also be used with remarkable dexterity to handle large and tiny foods, peel peaches, open door latches, unscrew jar lids, flick feathers into the air, pick nuts from small pine cones, and delicately manipulate other small objects. Naturalist Enos Mills, describing a grizzly bear in *The Spell of the Rockies,* wrote, "I constantly marveled at . . . [the] lightness of touch, or the deftness of movement of his forepaws."

Bears' fur, thick over their body and consisting of short to long hair, is an extremely effective insulation. There are no obvious external differences in sexes, though females of a species are typically slightly smaller and lighter.

They are intelligent, independent, and self-sufficient wild animals, possessing incredible instincts, and are quite adaptable, especially the American black bear, to environmental changes. Their senses of smell, hearing, and vision have become highly developed during their evolution. Generally, finesse is a trait of black bears, while the brown bears rely more on power. Brown bears are basically shy, though when necessary more aggressive than black bears, while the latter are more likely to enter the realm of people. Both species are capable of matching wits with people.

Distribution and Populations

Bears have been evolving for about 40,000,000 years; today's bears descend from a family of small tree-climbing carnivores. Fossils of the Hemicyon, or half-dog, found in the rocks of the Miocene epoch, display the physical characteristics of both bears and dogs, and indicate the related evolutionary descent of wolves, hyenas, weasels, other wild dogs, and bears. *Ursavus elemensis,* the oldest true bear, was the size of a fox terrier.

American black bears are the most common species of bears, distributed in forty-two of forty-nine states (bears have never existed in Hawaii), in eleven of the twelve Canadian provinces and territories, in which they originally occurred, and in five (possibly four other) states of Mexico.

Kodiak bears (a sub-species of brown bears) are isolated on the Alaskan islands of Kodiak, Afognak, and Shuyak. The coastal brown bears (grizzly bears) of Alaska are larger than the inland grizzly bears and are considered Alaskan brown bears.

Grizzly bears are found in Idaho, Montana, Washington, Wyoming, Alaska, and the Canadian provinces of Alberta, British Columbia, the Yukon Territory, and the Northwest Territories. Having adapted to wide ranges of temperature and climate, they normally inhabit a broad variety of country.

There are approximately 340,000 American black bears in the United States and more than 370,000 in Canada. Brown bears (including grizzly bears) number approximately 44,000 in the United States (mostly in Alaska, with little more than 1,000 grizzly bears in the lower forty-eight states). Canada has approximately 22,500 grizzly bears.

The Species

American Black Bears (*Ursus americanus*)

The smallest bears of North America, the bears we have come to love—the clown, the beggar, the bears of the na-

American Black Bear   *Courtesy Yellowstone National Park*

tional parks—are our most common and troublesome bears. American black bears have straight, Roman noses, short hair, lanky builds, and short, hooked claws. Logically named by the early settlers of the East Coast of North America, where these bears are nearly all black, they are widely varied in coloration across the continent: black; all shades of brown; blond; a white subspecies (Kermodei bears of British Columbia); blue-gray subspecies (glacier bears of Alaska and Yukon Territory); and sometimes a white V-shaped throat or chest patch. The color of an individual is relatively uniform, and a brown snout is the norm for all of this species. The average weight of black bears is 250 pounds, with a range of 125 to 600 pounds. The black bears of eastern North America are consistently larger than those of the western states, provinces, and territories. They live an average of eighteen years.

Brown Bears (*Ursus arctos*)

These are the most widely known species of bear, primarily due to the notorious and controversial grizzly bear (a subspecies) and the overall size of the species. They possess a dished-in face with a high brow, and short, round ears (set more forward on the skull than those of the black bear) that are small compared to the skull. They are enormous in size, with a strong build, great strength, thick head, and a large distinctive hump of fat and muscle over the shoul-

der. Long guard hairs on the hump enhance this important feature of identification. Their claws are straight, and
quite long on the front paws. Their color is variable,
though generally various tones of brown, and the color of
individuals is relatively uniform.

Kodiak Brown Bears (*Ursus arctos middendorffi*)

Dignified, majestic and solitary, Kodiak bears are massive,
with an average weight of 725 pounds and a range from
500 to 900 pounds. Their average life span is twenty years.

Alaskan (Kodiak) Brown Bears   *Courtesy United States Fish and Wildlife Service*

Grizzly Bears (*Ursus arctos horribilis*)

Grizzly bears have long been the most celebrated of all bears of North America, having captured the attention and imagination of people due to their size, temperament, and deadly conflicts with humans. They are feared not

Grizzly Bear   *Fernandez & Peck/Adventure Photo & Film*

only because of many western legends, but also because of a considerable body of fact. Unlike other brown bears, they are quite diverse in color, which generally is brownish, but varies from blond to black, and lacks a uniformity in color on the body and head; the fur there often has a grizzled appearance (for which they got their name) due to silver-tipped guard hairs. A white collar at the throat and chest is not uncommon on cubs. Grizzly bears average 490 pounds, and range from 350 to 700 pounds. Their average life span is twenty-five years.

Strength, Agility, and Quickness

All bears possess enormous strength. The strength of a bear is difficult to measure, but observations of bears moving enormous rocks, carrying animal carcasses, removing large logs from the side of a cabin, tearing off a section of roof or wall from a house, bending an automobile door nearly double, and digging cavernous holes are all indicative of colossal power. No animal of equal size is as powerful. A bear can kill a moose, elk, or deer by a single blow to the neck with a powerful foreleg, then lift the carcass in its mouth and carry it for great distances. Ben East, in *Bears,* best describes this display of strength: ". . . a brown [Kodiak bear] . . . took a thousand-pound steer a half mile up an almost vertical mountain, much of the way through alder tangles with trunks three or four inches thick."

Strength, power, and leverage are not only the attributes of adult bears, but also the young. I have observed a yearling American black bear, searching for insects, turn over a flat-shaped rock (between 310 and 325 pounds) "backhanded" with a single foreleg. The bear was captured the following day in a management action and was weighed at 120 pounds.

Along with bears' strength and power comes a surprising quickness and agility. They can run at top speed, then instantly whirl and spin on a spot, and immediately be at top speed in the opposite direction. They react faster than a human is able to perceive.

Behavior

Disposition and Personality

Bears have a wide range of behavior, but generally are curious, suspicious, crafty, cunning, cautious, self-reliant, independent, and dangerous. The only certainty of a bear's behavior is unpredictability. More specifically, American black bears are extremely clever, easily food-conditioned, and creatures of habit, but also adaptable, inquisitive, and playful. Grizzly bears are generally shy and peaceful, secretive, and ferocious when provoked, while Kodiak bears are dignified, deliberate, fearless, bold, generally peaceful, and solitary. Grizzly bears become extremely aggressive when threatened, while black bears are more intimidated by humans in a similar situation.

Intelligence

Bears' intelligence is difficult to assess, and should not be compared to or measured in human terms. They are considered by scientists and naturalists to be highly intelligent animals, based on their ability to learn rapidly and to reason. They bluff, choose alternatives, avoid problems, and retreat in the face of great odds. They appear to have excellent memories, especially in relation to food sources or threats.

Curiosity, coupled with an excellent memory, may be the key to a bear's "intelligence." It leads to learning and knowledge, which is the basis of survival—adaptability to environmental changes and unusual circumstances. Bears learn and remember from a single experience—a food source, a threat, a trap, or a rifle shot. Terry Domico, in *Bears of The World,* writes:

> Bears are highly intelligent and individualistic and are capable of nearly as many responses in a given circumstance as a human. . . . Some biologists believe the highly adaptable brown bear is intelligent enough to be ranked with primates, like monkeys and baboons.

Studies at the University of Tennessee psychology department have found American black bears very intelligent, probably more so than many other mammals. They open door latches and screw-top jars, untie rope knots, and recognize uniforms and vehicles. On one occasion, two five-year-old American black bears ran to a group of humans for security when a larger bear arrived.

Bears have on numerous occasions used rocks to "spring" live traps, allowing them safe access to the bait. One female black bear outwitted biologists at least a half-dozen times by rolling a large rock onto the trap. Hidden snares were finally her downfall.

An account is related of a Russian brown bear imitating the call of an elk (moose are called elk in Asia) during the rutting season, luring the unsuspecting animal to where it would be easier prey.

Bears have been observed by biologists assessing situations and circumstances, reasoning, then making a decision. Outwitting a bear is not a certainty, but a challenge, as you might conclude from the following report in *Bear Attacks,* by Stephen Herrero, wherein State of Pennsylvania bear biologist Gary Alt describes tracking a black bear:

> The bright afternoon sun was melting the snow from the rocks, and he [the bear] began to use this to his advantage, jumping from rock to rock. He left little sign this way, making tracking much more difficult. After a while he reached even deeper into his bag of tricks and came out with something new—backtracking. . . . Suddenly, his track simply vanished. There were no rocks, no water, nothing to

conceal his tracks. My first thought was that he had climbed a tree. . . . I went back to the tracks. This time I noticed there were toe marks at both ends, even though there was no evidence in the snow to indicate the bear had turned around. I followed them back about 50 yards and found where the bear had jumped off the main trail, walking away in a direction perpendicular to his old tracks. He pulled this backtracking stunt on six separate occasions during the day, successfully slowing the tracker.

Curiosity

Bears' curiosity may be attributed to many things, but often a potential meal is the source. They will inspect odors, objects, and sometimes noises to determine if the origin is edible or possibly a plaything, or for reasons we do not understand.

Curiosity is often what brings a bear into the human world, to your residence, garage, ranch, vehicle, camp, or picnic site. "Young adult grizzly bears are particularly curious," according to Herrero, "and their curiosity is not yet tempered with a knowledge that humans can mean trouble."

Tom Walker, in *We Live in the Alaskan Bush,* relates an experience with a young bear: "The bear was a small one and had followed me out of youthful curiosity to see what manner of creature I was."

Senses

Bears augment their incredible physical attributes, intelligence, and intense curiosity with remarkable sensory powers. This combination makes them formidable opponents with whom to match wits. An understanding of bears' senses—their incredible ability to detect almost anything in their habitat—provides an important insight.

Vision

It was once believed that bears' vision was poor. Recent scientific investigations, though, have shown it to be reasonably good, possibly equal to that of humans. They are nearsighted, but recognize form and movement at relatively long distances, and their peripheral, color, and night vision are quite reliable. Bears approach objects due to their nearsightedness and stand upright to increase their sight distance. Some biologists have ventured that bears may seem as though they have poor eyesight, when it just may be that they do not trust their eyes as much as their noses.

Smell

A bear's nose is its key to its surroundings. Stephen Herrero, in *Bear Attacks,* writes that, "Smell is the fundamental and most important sense a bear has. A bear's nose is its window into the world just as our eyes are."

No other animal has greater acuity of smell; it allows the location of mates, the avoidance of humans and other bears, the identification of cubs, and the location of food sources. A bear has been known to detect a human scent more than fourteen hours after the person passed along a trail. Another bear was observed to travel upwind for more than three miles in a direct line to a deer carcass. An old Native American tale may best describe the bears' keen sense of smell:

> A pine needle fell in the forest.
> The eagle saw it.
> The deer heard it.
> The bear smelled it.

Although their keen sense of smell allows bears to detect humans, which they would normally prefer to avoid, their sensitive noses detect human food sources, as well. Often hunger overpowers judgment, and bears approach people, their facilities, and activities.

Hearing

Bears' sense of hearing is more sensitive than that of humans. They have been known to respond to the sound of a camera shutter, or click of a door latch, at more than fifty yards, and to detect normal human conversation at more than a quarter of a mile, and from within a house one hundred and fifty yards distant.

Pain

Bears experience pain stress from internal and external sources. Their pain should not necessarily be compared to that of humans, which is possibly more complex. Generally, they do not appear to display obvious reactions as humans do. Bears have numerous injuries because of the nature of their existence, and, according to Gerald Mernin, park ranger and bear manager in Yellowstone National Park, can be compared to professional football players who "live in a world of constant pain." Persistent pain produces irritability, resulting in many "problem" bears that display their discomfort by aggressive actions toward other bears and humans.

Hibernation

Hibernation is a state of dormancy and inactivity—a deep sleep—that is utilized by bears and various other animals to adapt to limited winter food supplies. It is not a response to cold; a bear's fur is as necessary inside the den as outside. Hibernating bears differ from other hibernators such as bats, marmots, squirrels, woodchucks, and rodents that fall into a true deep sleep. Bears' metabolic rates and temperatures do not drop to the low levels of these other animals, and bears may awaken during a warm period and move about outside the den, though usually remaining quite close.

Specific lengths of hibernation depend on climate, location, and temporary weather patterns, and on the sex, age group, and reproductive status of an individual bear.

Three Asian and the South American species of bears do not hibernate. Some black bears in the southern United States (Alabama, Arizona, Florida, Georgia, Louisiana, Mississippi, South Carolina, and Texas) may sleep only a few days at a time, depending on local conditions.

American black bears begin preparing their dens in September, entering late that month or in early October, and denning until late April. Normally, their dens are natural or man-made hollows or shelters on a slope with southern exposure; e.g., caves, under logs, under tree roots, under large boulders, culverts, under buildings, or well above ground in tree cavities (one tree den in Louisiana was ninety-six feet above the ground). They rarely dig their dens, though they may scrape out obstructing debris.

Brown bears begin preparing their dens during the same period as black bears, but enter approximately two weeks later, and emerge a short time later than the black bears. The dens of brown bears are primarily dug in dry earth, under large boulders or the root systems of trees. They are usually located on northern slopes, except for some of those dug by bears on the Alaskan peninsula. In the U.S. Rocky Mountains, 61 percent of grizzly bears den on a north-facing slope.

Reproduction

Bears are polygamous, and a single male may mate with several females. They court with demonstrative affection, acting very boisterous and voicing long, melodious calls. Andy Russell, in *Grizzly Country,* describes a male grizzly bear who "comes to pay court with the delicate finesse of an animated locomotive running on a one-way track."

Reproduction is similar among bear species, though some variations exist in the timing of reproductive and denning activities, reproductive rates, and litter size. Generally, the larger brown bears have less reproductive potential than the black bears. The number of litters a sow produces during her lifetime depends on her longevity, age of first litter, survival of litters (how soon she is able to breed again), and her individual health.

An American black-bear sow has her first litter at three to five years. She breeds during June or July, and in late January or February normally gives birth to two cubs, each weighing approximately a pound. A brown-bear sow is five years old when she has her first litter. She mates in May or June; grizzly bears may mate in July. Cubs are born in January or February, they, too, weighing a pound.

Motherhood

The drowsy hibernating mother, from the moment of giving birth, begins her long effort to ensure her offsprings' survival. She nurses her cubs for an average of 200 days, of which nearly half are spent in the den before coming out of hibernation in the spring. Nursing (lactation) is the greatest energy demand on a sow's body, and her search for food becomes more persistent.

A sow is fully and solely responsible for her young, "cub-bing" without fatherly assistance. Her primary concern is for her cubs' safety and education. She provides constant protection, and teaches the cubs how to survive alone. Where she visits, the cubs visit. If she finds food at your residence, the cubs are taught, and they remember that location as a future source of nourishment.

When a mother with cubs is confronted or threatened, she is one incredibly dangerous animal. Chapter 3 includes more about the danger of a sow with cubs.

Traveling

Bears travel constantly in search of food or a mate, or simply to investigate something that aroused their curiosity. In *No Room for Bears,* Frank Dufresne says, "No other four-footed animal in all the world travels so far in its lifetime."

Walking

Though these large wild animals seem to move with a lack-adaisical, shuffling gait, giving them the illusion of being slow and clumsy, they actually move with a splendid rhythm and precision. Bears are capable of negotiating almost any terrain, including the densest vegetation, extremely steep ridges and cliffs, and the swiftest rivers. George Laycock, in *The Wild Bears,* says, "The grizzly can barrel, tanklike, through thick brush that would bring a man to a complete halt." Bears are also capable of moving silently, though when on a hard surface, a grizzly bear's long claws make a scratching sound that very quickly gets your attention.

Bears are capable of standing upright, unaided, on their hind legs to observe, increase sight distance, fight, and to reach foods or prey. They are capable of bipedal locomotion, though usually for only a few steps.

Running

Amazingly swift, bears attain speeds of 25 to 40 mph— that's 50 percent faster than you—and are capable of outrunning Olympic sprinters. The stride of one galloping bear was recorded at seventeen feet between tracks. Although they can maintain their top speed only for short distances, their endurance is exceptional. They have been known to run without a break for ten miles, and they run uphill, downhill, and sidehill with speed and agility. A sow with two cubs traveled more than twenty miles through mountainous terrain in one hour. The danger and futility of running from a bear is obvious—you *cannot* escape.

Climbing

Young bears climb quite well, to feed, rest, play, or find safety. They climb naturally and don't need to be taught. Adult black bears are outstanding climbers, climbing regularly and easily to feed, escape enemies, or, in some areas, hibernate. Their climbing ability declines with age, so

older adults climb infrequently for food. Adult brown
bears (including grizzly bears) are poor climbers, though
not nonclimbers, due to their body weight and claw structure (long and straight, compared to the shorter, hooked
claws of black bears). Brown bears may also "ladder" up
trees with low branches and have ascended many feet
when necessary. This method allows the larger bears to
sometimes climb trees.

With this ability to climb, bears will negotiate trees to
reach fruit, to access a rooftop, or gain access into open
windows of buildings. They are capable of pulling themselves up onto any reachable ledge, window sill, low roof of
a building, or into a vehicle. They quite efficiently climb
up and over almost any fence where they can stand and
reach the top. Some have been known to conquer even
more formidable barriers.

Jumping/Leaping

Though unable to jump vertically from a standing start,
bears' horizontal leaps have considerable height. They are
quite capable of lengthy leaps towards prey or an aggressor, and a series of ten-to-fifteen foot long bounding leaps
is not uncommon.

Swimming

American black and brown bears are excellent swimmers,
strong and skillful, swimming for pleasure as well as food.

They appear to enjoy water, whether wading, splashing, soaking, lying, floating, sitting, scratching, or actually swimming. They swim "dog paddle" fashion and shake off water like dogs.

Bears not only enjoy wallowing in natural waters, but have on occasion bathed in swimming pools. A few times every year, residences in bear country, or closely adjacent to a bear's range, have unwanted pool guests.

Bear Habitat (Bear Country)

Bear country is any area or environment where bears live. This is where they find food, shelter, and the cover (vegetation) in which their movements are secure and secretive as they pursue prey and approach other food sources. Their habitat provides protection, mating opportunities, and denning sites. Black bears have adapted to various environments, including coniferous, mixed, and deciduous forests, high mountains, swamps, and meadows. Brown bears utilize the same types of forests, mountains and meadows, as well as tundra and tiaga. Both species live at elevations from sea level to nearly 10,000 feet.

Bears have home ranges, but are not territorial. They do not defend a territory from other bears, and the habitats of black and brown bears, and of individuals, overlap. The ranges of males are normally larger than those of females, and an adult female brown bear has a range two to five times larger than the range of an adult female black bear.

The movement of bears is in response to available food sources, and hierarchy may dictate habitat niches for sub-adults or family groups that avoid dominant male bears. In some cases, they are forced into poor habitat where they must seek or are attracted to unnatural and easily obtainable foods from areas of human habitation.

Foods and Feeding Habits

Bears, with the exception of polar bears, have evolved from a carnivorous ancestry to be the only large omnivores—they consume essentially anything and everything. However, all species appear to have preferences and seasonal needs, though most of their diet is controlled by the available and nutritious food sources of their habitat. Guided by their stomachs, these wanderers and opportunistic feeders are in a continual search for food, and they seldom feed very long in a single small area. Diverse gluttons, they scavenge, dig, prey, and remember locations of human food sources. Of all bear activities, the highest percentage of time is devoted to seeking food.

Brown bears consume considerably more foliage and roots and significantly less fruits and seeds than black bears. They consume more vertebrates than black bears, but carrion is eaten by both species, while brown bears, as expert fishers, have a passion for fish. Berries are an essential and common food for both species.

Digging is a necessity for bears, since much of their food is below the surface of the ground. Brown bears, including grizzlies, are formidable excavators, laying waste to enormous areas as they seek ground squirrels in their tunnels, nutritious roots, and corms. They dig dens and make channels under fences enclosing dumps. Black bears are capable of digging, though not quite as efficiently, as they do not possess the long claw structure of the brown bears.

Periods of Activity

American black and brown bears are normally active day and night, though in many locations human activities have caused them to adjust to a nocturnal livelihood, with some dawn and dusk movement. A few black bear populations have learned that unnatural—human—foods are available during the day, and have become more active during daylight hours. Some populations of brown bears, without as many human pressures, have for the most part remained diurnal.

Bears' movements are mostly predicated on their search for food, and therefore they are more active during periods of natural food shortages. They often increase their range or move to lower elevations in the fall in preparation for hibernation, or when there is a reliable source of human food.

So, what does all this mean? You may find bears active at any time of the day or night, depending on where you live, the availability of natural and unnatural foods, and the individual behavior of the bears. Remember, bears are unpredictable individuals. There are always exceptions, and there is no such thing as a "typical" bear.

Bear Sign

The recognition of bear sign is a critical element of living with bears—of determining the presence of bears and preventing a serious conflict. Bear sign comes in many forms, some readily recognizable and others more subtle and difficult to detect. It may be on the ground, a tree, a building, or another object.

Study and learn how to recognize the various signs left by bears. They will provide clues and warnings of bears' presence in your area of residence. Bear sign includes:

TRACKS   Tracks are among the primary signs; often there will be only partial tracks, and bears will not always leave visible tracks if the ground surface is dry and hard. Tracks will be five-toed, generally as long as a human's footprint but twice as wide. In the case of brown bears, toes closely together, foreclaw marks twice as long as the toe pads with tracks forming a relatively straight line. Black bear tracks have toes loosely spaced forming a curved arc, with claw mark

Grizzly Bear Tracks   *Courtesy Yellowstone National Park*

length not more than toe pad length (if visible).

SCAT Bear feces are often found around residences, in the yard or nearby, though they may be observed anywhere a bear has visited. The scats may be a mass of partly digested grasses, acorns, berries, insects, seeds, hair, pieces of bone, roots, wood pulp, fruits, human garbage, plastics, etc. The average sizes are roughly 2¼ inches (adult grizzly bear) and 1⅜ inches (adult black bear) in diameter, though size overlap occurs.

CLAW AND TEETH MARKS
Buildings, trees and other objects are often climbed, scratched, or bitten by bears as they explore areas or attempt to gain entry.

DIGGING The "plowing" of your garden, flower beds, or shrubbery is sign of bears seeking roots and vegetables; digging at the base of a building may be the sign of attempts to gain entry.

GRAZING AND BROWSING
Missing flower heads, or berry patches and fruit orchards that have been "picked," are signs of bear activity. (This could be a sign of deer as well.)

ROCKS Overturned rocks (natural and landscape), logs, and landscape timbers are signs of a bear searching for insects.

HAIR   Bears leave hair when rubbing against trees, wooden and wire fences, buildings, shrubs, brush, and other objects; hair may be found almost anywhere a bear has rubbed or closely passed.

DAMAGE   Buildings, equipment, and vehicles damaged; limbs broken from trees; livestock missing, injured, or killed; yard furniture and toys chewed and clawed—these are all signs of possible bear activity.

Day Beds and Shelter

Located near food sources and often with a commanding view, day beds are utilized by bears for resting. A bear may have several day beds throughout its range. Black bears sleep in trees, stretched out on limbs, or on the ground in grassy areas or on conifer needles. Brown bears use the ground, sleeping in grassy areas, on conifer needles, or in shallow depressions dug in soil or snow. Day beds are often located near residential and other developed areas.

TWO

Living in Bear Country

"Your best weapon to minimize the risk . . . is your brain. Use it . . . and continue to use it. . . ."
—Stephen Herrero, *Bear Attacks*

Living in bear country means just that—actually residing where bears live or frequently visit. Usually associated with wilderness, bear country also includes rural areas, such as isolated residences and lodges; small towns and villages; and other non-urban developments surrounded by bear habitat.

Bears also frequent residences and facilities immediately adjacent to their natural habitat, exploring suburban developments and the fringes of urban areas. On rare occasions, they will encroach well into the center of a large town or city.

Bear country is:

(1) Anywhere bears may inhabit on a regular basis—normal bear habitat.

(2) Areas where bears live temporarily and places they occasionally visit.

(3) And, for the purpose of this book, a few areas not normally considered bear habitat.

Ranges (an individual bear's normal area of use) vary in size according to food availability. When bear populations increase or natural food becomes scarce, some bears are forced to adapt and move into new and different habitat. These new locations are often inhabited by people, and the displaced bears find readily available nourishment in the form of human foods. As the bears become less afraid of people, these areas may become "home," a part of the food circuit.

A Philosophy of Living in Bear Country

The key to successfully sharing bear country with those who were here first is prevention of conflicts. That translates into preparation, and taking actions to eliminate the causes of the potential conflicts—matching wits with bears.

First, accept the fact that living in bear country entails additional responsibilities. Prepare for the inherent risks—personal risks—which are in no manner as great as the risk of traveling to and from home on the highways.

Second, be willing to undertake careful planning and preparation for the specific actions necessary to coexist with these highly intelligent animals. This endeavor must not be left to chance. "You conquer fate by thought," as Thoreau said.

With minimal human effort, bears and people can co-exist in their own niches without discord. Bear authority Paul Schullery notes, "Bears may be 'good' or 'bad' depending on how they fit the 'human plan.' "

A History of Living with Bears

People living in bear country is not a new phenomenon. In prehistoric times, through the ancient periods, and into the current era, people and bears have shared bear country.

Possibly the most dominant wild animals in human consciousness, bears have, through sharing the earth with humans, exerted distinct influences over them. Mythical, exciting, revered, human-like, and extremely dangerous, they have altered humans' behavior and consciousness.

Fossil evidence in caves and other deposits throughout North America, as well as in Europe and areas of Asia, indicates close associations between some of our primitive ancestors and "cave" bears. An unknown number of cave bears and early humans lived together, but our insight into the relationships between them is minimal and fragmented. With fossils, petroglyphs and pictographs, cave-wall art, bear-cave scratchings, and etchings of bears on stone and bone as our evidence, we have only a vague knowledge of prehistoric bears and people.

Very little is known of the association of the Cromerians and cave bears during the Late Pleistocene epoch, at least 700,000 years ago. Of course, at that time, the Eurasian continent was sparsely populated, with some regions uninhabited. Cave bears and our more recent ancestors, the Neanderthals (80,000–50,000 years ago) lived in what were close, but not necessarily harmonious associations. The Neanderthals and other nomadic groups were in conflict with bears, as they hunted—for food, clothing, tools—and destroyed them, and often were in turn killed. The Neanderthals used bear bones as art, ceremonial articles, and implements such as scrapers, clubs, and digging tools.

Reincarnation appears to have figured in the association between bears and the beliefs of early peoples, as bears entered the ground in the fall and returned to life in the spring. Bear cults existed, and bears were subjects of dances, rites, myths, and ceremonies. There were rites of burial, evidenced by caves with human and bear bones in ritualistic placement.

Crossing the Bering land bridge, American black bears came to North America about 250,000 to 300,000 years ago. The brown bears (present species) were a few years behind, entering the North American scene somewhere about 100,000 to 250,000 years ago. However, bears and people did not begin sharing this continent until about 35,000 years ago, when humans crossed this bridge from Asia. The early human associations with North American bears were not at all compatible, and bears were accorded treatment similar to that in Europe and Asia—they were pursued, hunted, and utilized.

The association, though, was definitely not one-sided in favor of humans. During that period, the giant short-faced bears (bulldog bears) existed. They were not only the giants of the Middle to Late Pleistocene epoch, but the largest carnivorous land mammals *ever*. They lived throughout North and South America. Powerfully muscled and gigantic, they measured more than five feet at the shoulders and over eleven feet tall standing, had a vertical reach of over fourteen feet (a basketball rim is ten feet high), and weighed one thousand five hundred pounds in the spring, more than a ton in the fall. Larger, but more slightly built than the Kodiak brown bears, they would make these present-day bears look like cubs. Extremely swift, the giant short-faced bears were the most powerful predators of their time. They kept black bears in trees and possibly humans temporarily off the North American continent. Unfortunately, this "bear's bear" was gone by the end of the last Ice Age, 11,000 years ago.

Bears in Ancient Times and the Middle Ages

Exploitation of bears throughout prehistoric times was honed in our ancient cultures and during the Middle Ages. Bears were the first zoo animals, probably due to being the easiest to keep. The Queen of Egypt, Hatshepsut, had a facility in 1500 B.C. that possibly could be considered the earliest zoo. Early Chinese rulers also had zoos, and King Ptolemy II of Egypt (285 to 246 B.C.) had a polar bear in a private zoo in Alexandria.

Bears were on display in Rome by 169 B.C. "Abuse" best describes the relationships between humans and bears during the Roman Empire, maybe more so than at any other time in history. Bears were for entertainment, but entirely expendable. They could be replaced from the seemingly inexhaustible supply of brown bears in the wild. The Romans considered them a symbol of power and strength, and included them in circus performances, chariot races, and warrior contests. The bears fought bloody battles with dogs, prisoners, or gladiators. They performed in large outdoor arenas such as the Circus Maximus, which held 150,000 spectators. Sometimes herds of bears fought packs of dogs.

The Roman Emperor Caligula, one of the most depraved and monstrous rulers of all time, used 400 bears during a single "games," and the Emperor Gordian, in A.D. 238, used 1,000 bears in a single event. The fights were to the death with the men, alone or as a group, using bow and arrow, sword, or spear. Competition was not always important, as there is evidence of a person with a spear facing six "snarling" bears, and prisoners were sometimes unarmed during the encounters.

Bears were a dominant element of Greek mythology. Divinities included bears as objects of ritual and immortality, and the mythology contained marriages of humans and bears to produce half bear-half human offspring. There were bear sacrifices to Zeus, the principle God of the pantheon and the ultimate ruler of the heaven and earth. Mythology has Zeus mating with the goddess Callisto, who at the time was a bear.

Bears were burned and otherwise sacrificed during ceremonies, and there were public executions and bear feasts. They were elements of art objects: pots, figurines, carvings, vases, and drawings.

Bears had enormous influence upon the peoples and the legends of the early Christian period. Numerous saints had strong associations and influences with bears, with some deriving their names from Ursus (a bear).

Bears in the Heavens

Bears have long been a part of our heavens. Polaris, the North Star, which we are taught to locate when very young and which was for so long the navigational monument of the Northern Hemisphere, is also known as Alpha *Ursae Minoris*. Two constellations, Ursa Major (the Great Bear) and Ursa Minor (the Little Bear), move counterclockwise around the North Star, which is the brightest star of the Little Bear. The "bear constellations" never set, and since at least the beginning of recorded history the Great Bear and the Little Bear, with the North Star, have guided explorers, travelers, and navigators in the north.

Bears of the Bible

The bear is often spoken of in the Bible, and has been considered a symbol of God's vengeance. In Lamentations,

Jeremiah sees God in His anger as a bear lying in wait, and in Revelation the dragon gave power to a beast with the feet of a bear. Possibly the most well-remembered bear episode is in the Old Testament, 2 Kings, when the prophet Elisha is mocked for his baldness by a large group of children. He curses the group, whereupon two "she bears" rush out of the woods and kill forty-two of them. Even Biblically, there was strife between bears and people.

Bears in Street and Circus Entertainment

Bears have entertained in the streets since the Middle Ages. They were muzzled, trained, and led around on chains for public amusement. In Egypt during the thirteenth century, marketplace entertainment displayed trained animals, including bears that "danced" or went to sleep when instructed. Their use in the streets continues today, as "sidewalk" bears accompany some of Eurasia's wandering musicians.

During ancient times, there was little if any belief in compatibly living with bears. They were used, and when a problem occurred in the wild or on display, they were killed. There was little consideration by the populace to accommodate bears that were a problem, particularly when the daily life of common folk was already horrendously burdensome.

Bears and Native Americans

As in other cultures, bears were pursued and utilized by Native Americans. The bear as a whole—skins, meat, fat, bones, teeth, other parts, and spirit—served many practical, medicinal, religious, and ceremonial uses. They were highly respected, considered supernatural, and often sacrificed, with an apology offered for the taking of their lives. Some groups respected bears with the belief they should not be sacrificed or hunted. In *Giving Voice To Bear,* David Rockwell writes about the association between bears and Native Americans:

> Bears and Indians have lived together on the continent of North America for thousands of years. Both walked the same trails, fished the same salmon streams, dug camas roots from the same fields, and, year after year, harvested the same berries, seeds, and nuts. Indians came face to face with bears when both coveted the same berry patch, for instance. . . . The relationship was one of mutual respect. But it went well beyond that. Bears were often central to the most basic rites of many tribes. . . .

The Native Americans' relationship with the "mysterious monsters" (grizzly bears) was, for the most part, one-sided. Although they revered, feared, and respected bears, many of these peoples were also aggressive toward them. Meriwether Lewis and William Clark, who spent considerable time with the Indians and encountered numerous bears during their travels across the continent, related that the Indians ". . . hunted . . . in parties of eight to ten men . . . [and] warriors wore war paint as they would when going to war against their [human] enemies."

Hunting and killing bears was a display of courage, carried out with substantial ceremony. Hunters believed bears were supernatural beings. Grizzly bears were considered powerful, and therefore guardians; black bears appeared weak, and were regarded as spirits.

Ceremonial reverence was the Native Americans' most notable relationship with bears, though their most deeply rooted feeling was fear. Bears were vicious; they mutilated and killed.

The lives of Native Americans involved initiations that included a variety of bear-related rituals and their supporting myths. Passage into men's and women's secret societies, puberty rites of girls, the initiation into manhood, and the induction of shamans all involved bears. They were considered guides between the worlds of spirits and humans, embodiments of the Indians' respect for natural things. Bears were also considered gods, and symbolized death and birth. A major belief existed that bears were humans reincarnated—emerged from hibernation—as human-like animals.

Some Native Americans believed the first Indians were the children of a bear and a woman. Grizzly bears were known as the "chief's son," "chief's daughter," "grandfather," "great grandfather," "elder brother," "great bear," and numerous other respectful names. Some Native American groups, regarding bears as relatives, would not eat their meat; some would eat black bears but not grizzlies.

There are considerable differences between living with bears today and in the past, but many of these beliefs, ceremonial practices, and ways of life continue among the Native Americans of North America. We should be thankful that they do, because it is a tragedy when we lose such important cultural practices and their history.

Bears and North American Explorers

As early as A.D. 985, explorers sailed along the East Coast of North America and undoubtedly observed American black bears. In 1540–1542, Francesco Vasquez de Coronado and his expedition traveled through American black-bear and grizzly bear country, in what are now Colorado, Kansas, Nebraska, and New Mexico. Pedro de Castaneda, a member of the expedition, wrote of "many bears."

Henry Kelsey, on August 20, 1691, noted grizzly bears in northwest Canada, when employed by the Hudson Bay Company. He provides the earliest known reference in the English language to a grizzly bear, according to Harold McCracken in *The Beast that Walks Like Man*. Kelsey wrote:

> To day we pitcht to ye outermost Edge of ye woods this plain affords Nothing but short Round sticky grass & Buffillo & a great sort of Bear wch is Bigger than any white Bear & is Neither White nor Black But silver hair'd like our English Rabbit. . . .

From the late 1600s, bear observations and recordings in North America correspondingly increased with new exploration, population growth, and expansion.

Bears and Eastern Settlers

Along the East Coast of the North American continent, early settlers encountered and named "black" bears. In 1602, the "first published record of bears in Massachusetts" was made, according to James Cardoza in *The Black Bear of Massachusetts.* The Native Americans of this region had long utilized the bears, and the early Anglo-American settlers followed with similar consumptive practices. Meat (considered "delicious eating"), oil, clothing, cosmetics, jewelry, and medicines were just a few of the uses of bears by the most recent residents of that period. Bear skins were valuable, and the furs were shipped from North America to Europe. In 1743 alone, 16,512 furs were exported, and such exportation continued, with more than 10,500 sent to England in 1783.

Bears were also considered pests by these early settlers, a definite annoyance. Cardoza notes that "Foolhardy settlers, contemptuous of the bear's abilities or puffed up with self-righteous bravado, attempted to overcome bears with such varied instruments as jack-knives, axes, oxgoads, pitchforks, and hoes."

The land was cleared for agriculture, and as forests diminished, so did bear habitat. Bears and humans conflicted in many ways, and the bear lost; persecution of bears continued as it had from the prehistoric beginning.

Bears and Early Western Settlers

The men and women of the frontier frequently encountered bears. Settlers had lived with bears—though in a most incompatible manner—and would continue to live with them as Americans pressed westward.

The lives of early settlers were marked by extreme hardship. Settling in a wilderness, eking out a livelihood, and always on the move, they attempted to establish roots—a home and the beginning of crops. Living in true subsistence style, some nearly starving, these early residents worked long and hard. They planted gardens and sowed crops; raised pigs, chickens, goats, sheep, cows, and horses. The result was disastrous when the opportunistic bears found these new cornucopias of readily available nourishment. Bears entered their corrals and pastures, killing, carrying off, and eating their livestock. They raided fields and gardens, not only consuming much of the corn, sugar cane, and vegetables, but trampling and destroying the crops as well. Unable to afford the inconveniences and losses wrought by bears, settlers killed them. These people did not have present-day knowledge and technology to prevent conflicts, nor did they have the inclination to bother with any action other than to eliminate the frightening marauders.

Bears and Mountain Men

Western expansion carried with it traditional attitudes and practices toward bears. During the 1700s and 1800s, mountain men—prospectors, miners, fur trappers, explorers—found bears wherever they ventured. As they moved into the Great Plains, they encountered grizzly bears. The mountain men found these residents to have little fear of them, or of anything, for that matter. These light-colored "white" bears were rulers. The adventurers had experience with black bears, but the grizzly bear presented a new challenge—it had a ferocity that prompted an intense desire to "tame and control."

The mountain men recognized the grizzly's awesome physical prowess, horrible disposition, and omnivorous eating habits. Respect, awe, and fear were a few of the emotions of these early residents of western bear country, but they considered themselves tough men, conquerors, and had to shoot any bear observed.

Well armed, especially in comparison with the Native Americans, the mountain men did not tolerate any threat or inconvenience posed by bears. Without much of an obvious reason, some early pioneers sought and attempted the extermination of this feared species, which they called Moccasin Joe, roach bear, Old Ephraim, or the monarch of the mountains. They killed grizzly bears just because they were powerful and large, because they existed, and because to kill one was a bragging feat. Hunters and trappers killed bears for their furs, miners eliminated them as pests, and most settlers used their parts and meat in daily subsistence.

The battle was not totally one-sided: many mountain men were attacked, mauled, and killed in their attempts to destroy bears. However, more and more bears of both species were killed, until the remaining four-footed residents of the regions learned to maintain their distance.

People continued to move westward into bear country—not only the mountain men, but settlers and other explorers. The bears were losing. There was no coexistence or sharing of the land, and the bears' survival meant withdrawing from any human presence, or at least to places without galloping horses, traps, and gunshots. Previously free to roam at will, bears were now relegated to country out of the range of the frontiersmen. A *coexistence of separation* was occurring. Old Ephraim was being persecuted. Bears did not necessarily retreat; they were being killed, and in most cases only those in remote areas avoided the oppression.

Bear Hunters

Although bears were killed by many people for a variety of reasons, "sport" was often involved. They were a challenge to hunt. During the nineteenth century, there was a unique element of hunters who lived in bear country to whom "outwitting" meant gaining the opportunity to shoot. They hunted as a profession, for subsistence, to help a friend, incidentally to another occupation, for sport, and even occasionally "in self-defense." They were of many professions and livelihoods: farmers, ranchers, blacksmiths, shoemakers, soldiers, U.S. Congressmen, trappers, a valet, a U.S. Senator, civil engineers, a school principal, and carpenters. Some were wealthy, a few poor; one was a California aristocrat, while another had been a slave. Bears were a special quarry that offered trophies and bragging rites. Many hunted only black bears, while others living or traveling into the Great Plains and farther west sought grizzly bears.

Some of the "greatest" bear hunters lived and hunted from the early 1800s into the early 1900s: Ben Lilly, Theodore Roosevelt, Davy Crockett ("did in" 105 in a six-month period), Wade Hampton III, Grizzly Adams, Jim Bridger, Robert Bobo (killed 27 in a single day), Tom Locke, and Moses Leonard. One whose life story stands out is Holt Collier, slave, Confederate soldier, and valet. He was directly responsible for or assisted in killing more than 3,000 bears. Author Paul Schullery, in *The Bear Hunter's Century,* includes a statement by Collier from an April, 1909 issue of *The Saturday Evening Post* that may provide a small look into the life of a resident bear hunter:

> Didn't do nothin' much 'cept hunt. I would kill on an average one hundred and twenty-five to one hundred and thirty and one hundred and forty bear in a season. I reckon I have kilt more bear than any

man in the whole entire world. I kept count of 'em
up to twenty-one hundred. . . .

Collier, Crockett, and the others listed above are only a few
of those who enjoyed "the hunt." Their stories are intriguing—they relate such varied lives and philosophies—and
are well worth pursuing and reading.

Bears, Ranchers and Farmers

*". . . [T]he ranchmen came in with great herds of cattle and horses
and flocks of sheep, and built their log cabins and tilled their scanty
garden-patches, and cut down the wild hay for winter fodder."*
> —Theodore Roosevelt (from *American Bears,* by Paul
> Schullery)

Ranchers with large herds of livestock had a near-zero tolerance for the loss of a single head of cattle, horses, or
sheep, and were well equipped with ranch hands and
firearms to eliminate bears. With their cowhands, they
trapped and hunted them, eliminating any potential
predator on the range. Bounties were placed on bears and
the result was their destruction, and actual extermination
in many areas. William Wells, in the January 7, 1899 issue
of *Forest and Stream,* writes:

. . . but along about '89 [1889] the skins took a
jump in price, and at the same time some of the
Western States put a bounty on bruin. This made
hunting them profitable, and they commenced to

decrease rapidly. . . . [N]ow, when every bear, cubs and all, were worth $10 apiece, the poor brutes had no rest.

With little or no tolerance for these much-feared and destructive animals, ranchers developed a passion to kill them. There were even instances of killing cubs with rocks. But cattle-killing bears and the subsequent bounties were nothing new. Edward Topsell, in *The History of Four-footed Beasts* (1607), wrote about the problem: ". . . kill their Cattel left at large in the field in the day time; They likewise shoot them with guns, giving a good sum of money to them that can bring them a slain Bear."

However, a few bears were not easily killed, but continued to outwit ranchers and hunters. One such bear was "Old Mose," a Colorado grizzly bear of legendary status. Naturalist Enos Mills, in *The Grizzly*, describes the chaos wrought by this outlaw bear:

He regularly killed cattle, horses, sheep, and hogs. . . . Mose killed at least five men and eight hundred cattle, together with dozens of colts and other live stock. . . . Often he smashed the fences that were in his way. He had a fiendish habit of slipping upon campers or prospectors, then rushing into their camp with a roar, and he evidently enjoyed the stampedes thus caused. On these occasions he made no attempt to attack. Although he slaughtered stock to excess, he never went out and attacked people. The five men whom he killed were men who had cornered him and were attempting to kill him. . . . For thirty-five years he had kept up his cattle-killing depredations. During this time he was often seen and constantly hunted, and numerous attempts were made to trap him. . . . Two missing toes on his left hind foot were the means of identifying his track. . . . A heavy price on his head led the most skillful hunters and trappers to try for Old Mose. Three of the best hunters were killed by him. All trapping schemes failed; so, too, did attempts to poison. Finally [in April, 1904] he was cornered by a pack of dogs, and the hunter ended his career with the eighth shot.

Farmers, settling the western areas of the continent from the mid-1800s to the early 1900s, planted crops, including corn, other grains, and an assortment of vegetables, all which bears found to be readily available and nourishing food sources. Bears had to be killed to protect these crops, and as before, there was no harmony in bear country. In *The Wild Bears,* George Laycock related:

As long as bears and men have shared the earth, there has existed between them a special adversary condition. Although we sometimes ignore the small wild animals around us and let them go their way, the bear is a special case. Until recent years we have, almost universally, looked upon these animals as if they somehow threatened our territorial dominance.

By 1908 black bears were eliminated from seven of the forty-nine states in which they originally occurred and from one Canadian province. By 1935, grizzly bears were gone from fourteen of their original seventeen states, and two of the original six Canadian provinces and territories. Although long considered gone from Colorado, a grizzly was killed in 1979, and is now considered "the last one." Grizzly bears have since immigrated into Washington from Canada. Black bears may have been gone from some of the New England states, but have since reestablished themselves.

A Violent Coexistence

Stories of people living in bear country are exciting, tragic, often embellished, frequently humorous, and almost always about a huge, dominant, frightening animal. They are stories of human existence in a harsh world, of exploration and survival, and a history of our common residency with bears. As David Brown and John Murray reflect, "bear stories speak to the timeless battle between the human race and nature, and to the bear's singular status as nature's supreme symbol in the Northern Hemisphere."

Living with Bears Today

The attitude of people toward bears has changed in the last thirty-five to forty years. There has been an important realization that we might lose these incredible animals. As

Aldo Leopold, in *A Sand County Almanac*, explained, "Like winds and sunsets, wild things were taken for granted until progress began to do away with them."

Today, American black bears exist in forty-two states, nine provinces and two territories of Canada, and nine states of Mexico. Populations are increasing in many areas.

The following states and provinces have populations of black bears:

United States

Alabama	Massachusetts	Oregon
Alaska	Michigan	Pennsylvania
Arizona	Minnesota	Rhode Island
Arkansas	Mississippi	South Carolina
California	Missouri	South Dakota
Colorado	Montana	Tennessee
Connecticut	Nevada	Texas
Florida	New Hampshire	Utah
Georgia	New Jersey	Vermont
Idaho	New Mexico	Virginia
Kentucky	New York	Washington
Louisiana	North Carolina	West Virginia
Maine	North Dakota	Wisconsin
Maryland	Oklahoma	Wyoming

Canada

Alberta	New Foundland	Quebec
British Columbia	Northwest Territories	Saskatchewan
Manitoba	Nova Scotia	Yukon Territory
New Brunswick	Ontario	

Brown bears (B) and grizzly bears (G) presently live in five states and four Canadian provinces and territories:

Alaska (B, G)	Idaho (G)	Washington (G)
Alberta (G)	Montana (G)	Wyoming (G)
British Columbia (G)	Northwest Territories (G)	Yukon Territory (G)

Bear populations are managed, with bears no longer considered pests, but game or protected animals. People are more knowledgeable about bears, their attitudes have changed, and with only a few exceptions, they have learned to adjust their lives and attitudes, and to prevent conflicts.

Three
Conflicts with Bears

"We do all stand in the front ranks of battle every moment of our lives; where there is a brave [person] . . . there is the thickest of the fight, there the post of honor."

—Henry D. Thoreau (From *Thoreau On Man & Nature*, compiled by Arthur Volkman)

Basically reserved, bears would normally prefer to remain distant from people, but residents commonly attract them with foods and domestic activities. Some people's activities take them into wild places and into the presence of bears. Regardless of how bears and people meet, the result is often conflict—property damage, or, if a bear is surprised or feels that its space, food, or cubs are threatened, personal injury or worse.

An *encounter* may be a relatively close observation or meeting with a bear—close enough to be exciting, but not necessarily a conflict. However, a *conflict* between people and bears portends a serious situation, one caused by the behavior and requirements of each. It may be a face-to-face confrontation from which the bear flees, leaving the person to retreat or just stand there with a pounding heart. Such a conflict has enormous potential for serious consequences.

Worse, conflicts may lead to aggressive property damage by a bear or an attack resulting in serious physical injuries. For the purposes of this book there are three types of conflicts: close encounters, property damage and loss, and personal injury and death.

Provoked or Unprovoked Conflicts

People encroach on bears' territory with their activities and interests: clearing land; building roads, houses, mountain cabins, lodges, tennis courts, and swimming pools; and establishing ranches and farms. They bring with them lifestyles, food, and possessions that attract bears. The bears' behavior is altered, and they are provoked into actions and reactions that result in conflict.

Is there such a thing as an *unprovoked* conflict? What humans might consider unprovoked is always provoked as far as a bear is concerned. The reasons for its actions, though, are not always apparent to us. Unknown to us, a bear may have been forced by dominant bears into inferior habitat near residential areas. To survive, it must then use these areas, remaining close to people, with their attractants and presence becoming a provocation. Or a bear may be in such poor physical condition, or so starved, that it seeks any possible source of nourishment, including human foods and garbage. A bear's actions may be predatory; hunger might drive it to regard humans as food. Certain human actions can trigger a bear's predatory mode.

I believe that all conflicts between bears and humans, including attacks, are provoked by people, even if by our presence alone. Therefore, we have the ability to prevent conflicts. Larry Kaniut, after analyzing hundreds of bear attacks, reached this conclusion in *Alaska Bear Tales:* "Every bear has a reason for attacking. . . . [There is] no such thing as an unprovoked attack."

Causes of Conflicts

People come into contact with bears by two means: their actions take them to a bear, or a bear arrives in people's living situations. Each has the potential for conflict.

Attracting Bears

People knowingly and unknowingly surround themselves with a broad variety of bear attractants—odors, sounds, and objects that might be sensed by bears, resulting in their attraction to the source. Items capture the interest of bears for a single reason: they represent a source of food, a reward. Food can completely change their behavior, causing them to become more aggressive and bold. Conflicts with bears are normally associated with human foods, or with the most common attractant—garbage.

The number of conflicts varies from year to year according to the quality and quantity of natural foods. During a year when natural foods are readily available, bears tend to remain out of sight, but they may be in continual strife with people during a year of scarcity. Bears may become visually conditioned that certain objects or situations result in a food reward, e.g., an ice chest left outside a garage door, children playing in the yard (sound may play a part in this scenario), a vehicle parked outside, or any other item that at one time provided food. And, like dogs, some bears may simply be attracted to anything that "smells."

Occasionally, bears are interested in objects such as a swimming pool or a children's swing set in the yard. Their interest may stem from mischievousness, curiosity, or playfulness, though food certainly remains high in their priorities.

The list of possible attractants includes virtually anything you might have around the house or in the yard. Any of the following might attract a bear:

Animals (roadkill)	Berries
Aviaries (birds)	Beverages
Barbecue grills and accessories	Bird feeders and bird feed
Bear foods (natural)	Candles
Bee hives (bees, bee larvae, honey)	Candy and gum
Charcoal starter (liquid)	Garbage cans

Chemicals (stored and spilled)

Children

Children's activities

Children's play equipment

Cigarettes

Compost

Cosmetics

Deodorant

Dogs

Farm crops

Fish

Fish ponds

Flowers

Foods

Food freezers

Food lockers

Food odors

Food crumbs and scraps

Fruits

Game meat

Garbage

Petroleum products

Grains (crops, spills)

Gunshots

Gut piles

Household utenils

Ice chests

Insect repellent

Lawn furniture

Lawns

Livestock (cattle, horses, hogs, etc.)

Livestock (chickens, rabbits, etc.)

Livestock carcasses

Livestock foods

Meat smokers

Medicines

Mineral licks (natural)

Nuts (crops)

Oil filters

Paints

Patio furniture

Pets

Pet foods

Stills (moonshine, mash)

Plastics (toys, furniture, etc.)	Swimming pools
Recyclables	Toothpaste
Refrigerators	Trash
Salt blocks	Vegetables
Sewage	Wildlife carcasses
Spills (foods, chemicals)	Wildlife food caches

In *Our National Parks,* John Muir reflected upon bears' compatibility with the land and diverse eating habits, noting that, "almost everything is food except granite."

Bears will take all possible measures to find a reward. You may think that you have attractants well secured, only to have a bear utilize its incredible strength to remove a closed and locked door, break in or pull out a window, or even tear a hole in a wall. Black bears have been known to gain entry to a house by opening a door, pressing the latch or using both paws to turn the doorknob. Bears are fast learners. The damage they create is often extreme. Other, more serious, conflicts may occur if a bear encounters a resident and is surprised or feels threatened.

Surprising Bears

Surprising a bear is an immediate and common cause of a conflict, though it is usually preventable. Bears are normally shy and most often will move away when aware of you, though if accustomed to people, and conditioned to their food, they may remain in the vicinity. People who move silently through bear country, without providing any warning, run the risk of surprising a bear. Without letting your presence be known at a distance, and by failing to be alert to your surroundings, you can find yourself in a close confrontation that causes a bear to perceive a threat. The result is a surprise encounter—a serious conflict.

Entering a Bear's Critical Space

How do you feel when someone talks to you with his face only six inches away from yours? Uncomfortable? That person has invaded your "critical space." Bears, like humans, have a "space," an area around them in which they feel threatened when it is encroached upon. A bear's critical space may be five feet, twenty feet or a quarter of a mile—nearly any distance, depending on the individual bear and circumstances. In other words, you can't begin to guess what the space is. Instead, you have to warn bears so they can move away.

When a bear is approached too closely, whatever the distance, its reactions to the encroachment will depend on its individual temperament and mood at that moment. It may display a nonaggressive response or, in many such situations, an aggressive one. Whatever the reaction, it may not necessarily be due to surprise, as it may have been well aware of you for some time, but wasn't bothered until you violated its area of comfort.

A bear protecting a food source, even something it has found outside your back door or in your garage, will defend its prize when it feels you are a threat to that reward. Any intrusion into the protective space of a sow with cubs nearly always results in a major conflict with, at the least, serious injury.

Encountering a Protective Mother Bear

A mother with cubs is typically the most dangerous bear. Normally placid, but extremely alert, a sow considers motherhood—the education and protection of her cubs—her paramount objective. She is affectionate, devoted, constantly protective, and aggressive toward threats, real or *perceived*. She defends her cubs to whatever degree she believes necessary, bluffing or attacking until she has lessened the threat to her young. Nothing prompts a full-blown charge by a mother bear more quickly than the bawl and commotion of a cub. And nothing prompts a loud bawl from a cub more quickly than the presence of a person.

Bear Predation

Bears naturally prey upon wild animals, but not people. However, a bear may be in such poor physical condition, so starved and unable to secure natural foods, that it seeks any possible meal. A person's actions may trigger a bear's predatory mode. Predation on humans is extremely rare, but there are documented incidents of bears, mostly black bears, preying on people.

I relate here in my own words a story originally told by James Gary Shelton in *Bear Attacks: The Deadly Truth.*

A few years ago, 1994, in British Columbia, Canada, a family experienced a horribly tragic incident. Living in bear country, they took the necessary precautions to prevent the attraction of bears. However, not all residents of their small rural community did the same. A black bear had been seen in the area for at least three weeks, and reportedly had been fed. The bear was apparently habituated—unafraid of people—and conditioned to human foods, especially in light of the fact it came into this family's yard in the middle of the day.

On this quiet afternoon in mid-September, the mother was at home with her kindergarten-age son. He was playing with a small ball just outside a door of the house, on an above-ground deck. Watching out the window, she was aware when the ball went off the deck into the yard, and that her son climbed over the railing and bench onto the grass in pursuit. As she observed what appeared to be a black dog moving across the yard, she heard her son call for her. Hurrying to the railing and reaching over to assist him, she saw a black bear "bounding" toward them. Grasping her son, she was lifting him up over the railing by his shoulders when the bear grabbed the boy's side, pulling him from his mother's grasp. She was immediately off the deck and kicking the bear, screaming and hoping for help. She beat on the bear with a shovel, breaking the handle, hit it with a potted shrub, and a fish tank filled with dirt. Her child was being mauled—terribly injured. Now, without weapons, the desperate mother jumped on the bear's back, reached forward and wrenched at the bear's eyes. The bear dropped the boy and initiated an attack upon the mother, and what ensued was basically a "hand to hand" battle. Her screams were heeded, and help arrived in the form of several neighbors. The bear eventually ceased its attack, but remained in the yard in an extremely agitated mode, as the mother and her son were rushed to medical assistance. The young boy died. His mother, who fought so desperately for her son, and his father live with an indescribable loss.

The incident occurred in a location where you might expect to find a habituated and food-conditioned bear. Time of day did not seem to be a factor. The small boy had not surprised the bear, nor had he entered into its space. Possibly the boy's actions, and size, fit the predatory blueprint, triggering the tragic response. Preventing such attacks is the ultimate reason for outwitting bears.

A Combination of Situations and Factors

The ingredients of a conflict are a combination of any one of two situations and any one of five factors.

Situations:

Bears and people come together because people attract bears to human locations and activities.

Bears and people come together because the humans' activities take them to where the bears are at that moment.

Factors:

People surprise bears.

People enter into bears' critical space.

People pose a threat to sows and their cubs.

People pose a threat to food sources that bears are guarding.

People are preyed upon by bears (rare).

There may be more than one factor involved in a situation. For example, a person surprises a sow with cubs, or enters the critical space of a bear guarding food, or maybe the ultimate—surprises a sow with cubs while she is guarding a food source.

Habituation and Food Conditioning

Many attractants will bring bears near humans, but the true rewards are human, pet, bird, and livestock foods, including garbage. Procuring natural foods is a constant, time-consuming, and difficult process for bears. Most of their day involves the search for food. How can they not be thrilled with finding a readily available, consistent, and high-calorie source of nutrition? As they find and eat foods provided by humans, bears become conditioned to this easily obtained source of nourishment. They remember the specifics of each source of food, such as location, time, and any threats they encountered. They also appear to reason that if humans provide food at one source, then humans everywhere can provide food. As part of this process, bears lose their fear of people and are more likely to approach and seek food from your part of bear country. The become *habituated* to people. The result of habituation and food conditioning is an enormous potential for conflict, which can lead to property damage, personal injury (sometimes death), and frequently the death of the bear.

An Alaskan sled dog owner related a story that not only depicts food conditioning, but is a vivid example of the failure of dogs to deter a bear. The dogs were chained to posts outside their respective dog houses in the kennel area, which is approximately fifty feet from the house. A large grizzly bear, paying no attention to the thirteen frantically barking dogs (two or three were cowering in their houses), walked within six feet of several of the dogs as it went directly to the back door of the house, where it had previously broken in and obtained food. The dogs were no deterrent whatsoever to this food-conditioned bear as it returned to a known food source. The bear was eventually destroyed.

Property Damage and Personal Injury

The loss of foods or animal feed is the least of people's problems when bears are attracted to their homes and activities. Bears inflict enormous damage as they attempt to obtain attractants. Bears looking for food damage windows, doors, furniture, barbecues, boats, vehicles, garbage containers, food freezers, crops, bird feeders, and beehives. Pets and livestock are killed. Bears even soil carpets and floors by defecating and urinating. Their exit from a building is often by a different route than their entrance, providing further damage.

A bear's enormous strength enables it to inflict incredible damage to almost anything. Larry Kaniut, in *Alaska Bear Tales*, relates a U.S. Forest Service employee's description of a brown bear's visit to a cabin in Alaska:

> He sledge-hammered the door open. . . . All . . . windows had been knocked out from the inside with sufficient force to ruin the window frames as well as to break the glass. The . . . cabinets had been torn from the wall and reduced to kindling, and the edge of the table looked like fancy lace where dainty bear-sized bites had been taken from

Residential Garage Door Damaged by a Bear Seeking Access to Human Foods
Courtesy Kevin Frey, Montana Department of Fish, Wildlife and Parks

around the edge. The stovepipe was chewed up and wadded into metal gobs and although stove parts lay scattered . . . the stove was gone. It was later found in about six feet of water at the edge of the lake. . . .

Conflicts with bears can have a high cost. According to the New Jersey Division of Fish and Wildlife, during 1999 there were 1,659 bear complaints resulting in $250,000 worth of damage. Bears were responsible for 29 home break ins and numerous pet and livestock kills, as well as cornering and chasing residents, including children. New Jersey's bear population is quite small—only about 1,000.

According to the Wisconsin Department of Natural Resources, in a two-day period at a Wisconsin farm, a black-bear sow and her cubs inflicted $35,000 in damage to the trees in an apple orchard.

According to the California Department of Fish and Game, during 1998, a small community in California had nearly 1,600 incidents of damage by bears, resulting in $659,000 in damage.

Conflicts between bears and humans have costs beyond immediate damage. Bears that become habituated and food conditioned are problems that eventually require the "direct management" of wildlife agencies. The bears must be captured and relocated to remote areas, usually with a helicopter. Relocations are not always successful, and multiple attempts are necessary.

Bear-management actions are extremely costly. The British Columbia, Canada, Ministry of the Environment spends more than $1 million a year resolving conflicts with bears. All of these costs are borne by taxpayers. The total cost is not only money that could be used for other public projects, but also time that could be spent on other public services. Outwitting bears is well worth the minimal effort required by you.

If attacked, people will assuredly suffer injuries, mental trauma, and possibly death. Attacks, the ultimate encounters with bears, are uncommon, though several occur in North America every year. Bear attacks, with people's actions and reactions, are addressed in chapter 5.

The Cost to Bears

Bears attracted to people and their property are at risk. They may be struck and killed by vehicles along roads, or by trains on railroad right-of-ways. More commonly, though, bears become persistent problems, and when all attempts fail to relocate them, they are eventually killed. This is a sign that people have not met their responsibilities to protect bears by outwitting them.

A bear's death is a loss to a natural system that relies upon them as part of nature's balance, and a loss to the people to whom bears are economically and culturally important. Seeing a bear in its natural state is a highly memorable experience for many people, and even a single bear missing from a population diminishes that opportunity.

Outdoor Activities in Bear Country

Many outdoor activities have the potential of conflicts with bears, but precautionary measures can prevent those conflicts. So often, people are not prepared "bearwise" for a quick run or jog, a short walk, a bicycle or horseback ride, or a few casts at the local pond or stream, because they will be near home. You must consider bears to be *anywhere and everywhere* in bear country.

The following activities, all of which can take place close to home, can provide opportunities to surprise or enter the critical space of a bear.

Hiking, Walking and Jogging

These are normally solo activities that enhance the possibility of surprising bears or entering their critical space. Any path, trail, or roadside where travel is easy for people is also preferred by bears, and such places commonly bring the two species together. But hikers often encounter bears off-trail too, so remain vigilant wherever you are. Remember, a jogging pace will place you into a bear's space more rapidly than walking or hiking will. If there is bear sign in the area of your activities, alter the routes where you hike, walk, and jog.

I had an interesting, and baffling, series of encounters with a bear a few years ago. While on my daily runs, and always while making a considerable amount of noise, I would cross paths with a grizzly bear. These encounters occurred at the same location every morning along a road near my residence. The bear would run across the road approximately ninety feet in front of me, disappearing into the dense vegetation, always from my right to left, and at nearly the same time each day. This occurred during more than half of my runs in a three-month period. I found no food source that might have attracted the bear to that location, nor was there a wildlife trail. I suspected there was actually fun involved in this bear's behavior, but I also harbored some thoughts that someday my presence might not be tolerated. Although I became more cautious on my runs, I should have altered my route.

Bicycling

Bicyclists are particularly vulnerable in areas with roadside bears. Many bicyclists have had disturbing experiences with bears, including being chased and virtually pedaling into bears along trails and roads. A bicycle is normally traveling at a high speed and is relatively quiet, providing the chance of moving into a bear's space suddenly, and therefore increasing the potential for a conflict. Bicyclists can attach a piece of cardboard (a playing card) to the bicycle frame where it will be struck by the spokes and provide an audible warning for a bear.

Horseback Riding

Travel with horses and other stock such as mules, ponies, burros, and llamas is quite common in some bear country.

Many residents and ranchers have stock, and riding stables are maintained by lodges and other guest facilities. People who use these animals have few bear encounters, as bears appear to easily detect stock, associate the animals with people, and keep their distance. But alertness and caution are necessary, even if just to prevent a bear from spooking a horse.

Berry and Mushroom Picking

Persons picking mushrooms and berries are quite vulnerable to close encounters with bears, as this activity places them amid some prime bear foods. Pickers often are so focused on the search and collection—head down, and sometimes on hands and knees—that they suddenly find themselves sharing a berry patch with a bear. Groups of pickers seem to have fewer encounters because of the noise they make, so be sure never to go picking alone. If a bear approaches you, drop your container of berries, regardless of how full it is, and retreat slowly. (Refer to "Bear Aggression" in chapter 5.)

Observing and Photographing Bears

Some of the more serious encounters with bears have occurred when people approached and crowded them while attempting to come within close range. You should view and photograph bears from at least 100 yards. Less than that is a risk, and more than 100 yards may still be a risk. If you see a bear from a long distance, enjoy it there and do not approach or attract it for a closer view. Use binoculars; photographers should use at least a 400-mm lens. Allow the bears to continue their activities. If they are near your residence, photograph from within the security of your home. If they approach your residence, you may want to make noises to discourage them. (Refer to "Bear Aggression" in chapter 5.)

Fishing

Lakes and streams are not only in bear country, but in some of the best bear habitat. There are endless opportunities for a person fishing to encounter a bear. Bears feed on vegetation in riparian areas along streams and the shores of lakes and ponds, and they also fish, usually where an abundance of fish—a spawn—makes the effort worthwhile. There may be a congregation of bears at a stream with heavy spawning, or a single bear seeking a lone fish in shallow water. Bears have been known to challenge a fisherman for their catch. If a bear approaches, wanting your fish, leave them on the ground and slowly depart. If a bear grasps a fish that is hooked and in the water, cut your line. Other wildlife often die along shorelines and their carcasses attract bears, and these locations are also excellent travel routes for bears and people. Fish entrails are quick to attract bears, so if you catch and keep fish, clean them at home.

Hunting

Your residential area may be one where hunting is a feasible activity. A hunter often moves silently and secretively through a variety of vegetation, including dense foliage, which greatly enhances the likelihood of surprising and crowding a bear, including a sow with cubs. Successful hunters carry bird or animal carcasses that are highly attractive to bears. A bird and small-game hunter is normally able to properly secure the kill by easily transporting it to a vehicle or residence, but a big-game hunter is faced with handling a large carcass that is a major bear attractant. Bears are also attracted to the kill site if there is a large quantity of blood, a gut pile, or the carcass. Some bears have learned that a gunshot means a gut pile or other rewards. Any of these attractants may bring a bear to the vicinity of your residence, or you may happen upon a kill site with an attending bear. If you find a bear on a carcass, and it is unaware of you, slowly and quietly depart. (Refer to "Bear Aggression" in chapter 5 for information on what to do if the bear *is* aware of you.)

Driving

Slow speed and considerable caution are required while driving in bear country. Every year, hundreds of bears in North America are struck by motor vehicles, resulting in the deaths of the bears, and nearly all incidents result in major damage to the vehicles. We are not talking about outwitting bears here, but about respecting them by driving more slowly and cautiously, especially at night.

A few incidents have occurred in which after bears were struck, the drivers got out of their vehicles and were attacked by the injured bears. A park ranger in Yellowstone National Park tells the interesting story of one such event: "An unbelievably foolish driver was charged by a sow when he got out of his vehicle to check the bear cub he had run over. He was miraculously able to retreat to the safety of his car, but the driver's door was demolished by the sow as the vehicle sped away."

In a unique example of "road rage," a very large grizzly bear was observed sitting in the middle of a two-lane road, on the center line, swatting at the passing vehicles.

Dogs

Dogs disturb and excite bears and are a cause of numerous encounters, whether at a residence or while a person is hiking, jogging, bicycling, or hunting. Whether a pet or a hunting dog, it may conflict with a bear by chasing it or barking, prompting a reaction from the bear. If the dog is not initially killed, it often retreats to its master, bringing along its new-found, irritated "companion." If a dog accompanies you in your bear-country activities, it must be leashed or otherwise well controlled. The use of dogs to deter and chase away bears is discussed in chapter 5.

How to Prevent Encounters

Alertness is paramount while participating in all of these activities. Keep your head up, looking ahead and around you. Too often, people travel with their heads down, more concerned with where they place their feet or bicycle tire than with what is around them. Try to balance your attention between the trail, road, or route and the country through which you are traveling.

The potential to surprise a bear along any avenue of travel is considerable. Bears use human routes to move from area to area. Design your travel to prevent surprising a bear, moving as much as possible in the open so that you can spot bears and give them the opportunity to evade you. Avoid dense vegetation, if possible.

Be on the lookout for bear sign. If you observe what you believe is bear sign, heighten your awareness. Identify the sign: has there been bear activity here? If so, you may wish to make a detour from your route, or even leave the area. Use extreme caution! Be alert and make noise.

Noise is your primary method of preventing surprise. Traveling in a group, or at least with a partner, provides the most natural and simple kind of noise—conversation. Talk about anything—just make lots of noise. Sing, yodel, or whistle (not a long, shrill whistle, but a more melodious tune). A strong wind in your face means that a bear you are approaching has less chance to detect you by sound and smell; therefore, increase your noise. The sound of your approach may be masked by the noise of moving water. Many people travel in bear country with noisemakers, not only bells, but pebbles in cans and whistles.

Four

Preventing Conflicts

"Whenever we go where the wild bear lives, we feel a keen sharpening of the senses, an unforgettable level of alertness."
—George Laycock, *The Wild Bears*

O utwitting bears requires the cooperation and efforts of many—individuals, families, agencies, businesses, and organizations. Everyone who lives in bear country needs to recognize potential conflicts with bears, understand the causes, and take preventive actions.

Outwitting bears is the responsibility of each family member, including children old enough to understand. A single omission by an individual may defeat the total family effort.

Bears must be outwitted early, because if they receive food, even only once, they will continue to seek rewards at that location, and they become considerably more difficult—often impossible—to deter.

Neighbors must be equally involved in preventing conflicts with bears. If one residence has a problem—attractants or rewards for bears—the potential for conflicts spreads to other homes and facilities.

Public Agencies

Many governmental agencies have bear-management responsibilities. Wildlife agencies are responsible for managing, conserving, and protecting wildlife, a duty that includes preventing injury, property damage, and the loss of bears, and promoting wildlife research and public education.

Wildlife managers will provide assistance to persons living in bear country, including measures to prevent bears from seeking and obtaining food and other rewards where people live. They have designs for deterrents such as bear-resistant structures and containers, and electric fences. Agencies also provide animal control, aversive conditioning, and the removal of problem animals. Some provide compensation for wildlife damage, including that by bears. Most wildlife agencies have brochures and other written materials about how to live with bears and other wildlife. They can also help you to avoid breaking the law.

Determine which agency is responsible for bear management where you live. Learn the names of the individuals working in your specific area, and become acquainted with them. Keep them aware of any bear activities and problems near your residence and living area, and seek their advice and guidance on living with bears.

If a conflict occurs, notify authorities immediately so that they can respond with appropriate management actions, including the rapid removal of a lingering problem bear. Failure to do so may result in additional and more serious conflicts—some quite tragic. Agencies investigate incidents and consider a variety of factors, including the history of an individual bear, whether the bear is a sow with cubs, the circumstances of the incident, the time of year, availability of natural foods, and available relocation sites.

As agencies strive to protect residents, their property, and bears, they may capture the bear by trapping or immobilization and then relocate it. Relocations are usually unsuccessful if a bear is conditioned to a specific food source, because a bear can navigate hundreds of miles back to where it was captured. Too often, a bear must be destroyed after a history of conflicts with people.

Wildlife-management agencies will do their very best to help you co-exist with bears. *Communicate and work with them!*

If current laws and regulations are inadequate for your protection and the preservation of bears, seek new legislation through your wildlife-management departments, legislatures, commissions, and other segments of government. Such efforts have provided many communities with improved sanitation systems—bear-proof garbage containers, enhanced garbage-pickup service, and longer hours of operation for sanitary landfills.

Where There Are People, There Is Food

Even if your efforts are working and you haven't had any problems, you must not become complacent. Maintaining a high level of prevention is essential. Remember, only a single reward for a bear is an incentive for it to return to the source. The animal is quite likely to seek rewards at other homes and facilities, as well. If food is available at once source, then, by bear reasoning, it must be available at all other similar sources.

An old adage, "Where there is smoke, there is fire," has been modified and adopted by bears. They quite accurately reason, "Where there are people, there is food!"

As bears wander in search of natural foods, it is only a matter of time, probably a very short period of random investigation, until at least one arrives in your area. If an attractant exists, *bears will investigate.* If the attractant is available, *they will be rewarded,* and if rewarded, most assuredly *they will be linked* to your area, home, and activities.

A Year-Round Effort

Because bears hibernate, we can determine, to a certain degree, the period of the year during which we are vulnerable to food-seeking bears. But our deterrent efforts should be a habit that we practice year-round. Maintaining these efforts during the winter is excellent prevention, since any sloppiness with food around the premises during the hibernation period might just be what attracts a bear when it emerges from its den in the spring. Remember, some bears in the southern United States do not hibernate much more than a couple of weeks, and even in the north, bears have been known to emerge during exceptionally warm periods of the winter.

Purchasing or Building a Home in Bear Country

Anyone purchasing or building a residence in bear country may first want to determine the history of bear problems in the area. Are houses broken into by bears? Is there an unsecured sanitary landfill, sewage-treatment plant, or slaughterhouse nearby? Are there bear trails on your prospective property that lead to and from these facilities? Is the house near a stream in which a lot of fish spawn? Is the area prime bear habitat? Are wildlife agencies involved in bear management in the area? Are they resolving the problems? Before you make a decision, know as much as possible about the area and its bears. Serious bear problems may be an excellent reason not to live in a specific area of bear country.

Preventing Conflicts in Residential Areas/Isolated Homes

In most conflict situations, no one control technique will provide absolute security from bear problems. However, certain measures that are initiated in a timely manner, maintained properly, and applied with an understanding of bear habits and behavior, can greatly reduce any problems associated with bears.

—Black Bear Conservation Committee,
Lower Mississippi Valley

Residences are the number-one source of bear attractants—foods, garbage, and other items that interest bears—with the possible exceptions of farms and ranches that have copious amounts of other attractants, in addition to the residential problems.

Houses and cabins are normally secure, and attractants are protected from bears, though odors are easily detected from outside. But determined bears can gain access to homes: they break windows, knock down or tear off doors, or pull siding off buildings. Once inside a residence, bears often damage anything they touch. They are known to destroy furniture and walls, and even to defecate throughout a home.

Even during unsuccessful attempts to enter, bears cause serious damage to residences. They have climbed onto and damaged roofs; crawled under houses and porches, and pulled out insulation; and torn screen doors from their hinges. One bear climbed onto a car, denting the hood, roof, and trunk lid as it gained access to a first-floor roof, where it stood and tore off portions of a second-story wall. Others have torn off the front-porch steps of a home;

broken windows; trampled flower beds; and inflicted considerable mental trauma to residents and their pets.

Open doors and windows not only improve a bear's detection of attractants, but provide them easy access to residences. Bears will walk directly through a door if it is open, or climb up through an open window. Screen doors obviously are ineffective in preventing a bear's entry, and screened porches and similar rooms are in no manner resistant to bears.

Mobile homes are not as strong as frame, brick and concrete structures, and are highly susceptible to bears breaking in. A black bear in southern Texas recently proved this point. The initial report was that a bear had broken into two isolated mobile homes and torn up "stuff" quite badly. Here is how Bonnie McKinney, a Wildlife Diversity Technician with Texas Parks & Wildlife, describes the culprit's actions:

> [The bear] had torn up screens on the porch, had been in one screen and out the other several times all around the front of the house, there were bear scats everywhere. . . . You would not have believed the mess he made. He broke out a window on the first trailer, went inside, and ate everything that he found . . . in a new gas refrigerator, which he demolished (cost $1800.00). He broke dishes, tables, chairs. Curtains [were] ripped, mattresses ripped, he didn't leave anything intact. Then [he] went to the

next trailer house, about fifty feet away. He couldn't get the door open, so he took the window air conditioner out of the window, then stood on it (his tracks were on it) and climbed inside through the window. He ate six boxes of D-con rat poison, flour, macaroni, noodles, sodas, fifty pounds of birdseed, and literally demolished the inside of this two-bedroom trailer house. He then went outside and tore the hot-water heater loose from the wall. He had practically lived in these two trailer houses for a couple of days. . . . He came back that night, and went to the shed where they kept tools and such and punctured several cans of motor oil.

Snares and other traps were set for the bear with no success, and there was no additional entry and damage at the homes. The bear had left the area, and McKinney decided to check a lodge about seven miles away. She further relates:

. . . [R]ight away we started seeing bear scats, full of garbage, birdseed and green rat poison . . . he had broken into this house also . . . he pulled the screens off the windows, but they were high, and too much trouble. So he . . . [went] to the front porch, pushed in a big plate glass window, [entered] and ate six more boxes of rat poison, bourbon, wine, sodas, flour and garbage.

The highly food-conditioned and habituated bear (we named him Iron Gut) was snared and immobilized at this location, and subsequently relocated to a zoo. According to McKinney, "He did have to undergo massive vitamin K treatments to get his liver enzymes back to normal after ingesting all the D-con rat poison."

The moral of this story is that mobile homes are readily entered by bears. All residences, especially mobile homes, must be clean and well sanitized, and have proper food and garbage storage to reduce odors, or a bear is going to pay a visit—and probably a not-too-delicate one.

TO OUTWIT: Usually, bears break into houses when they are unoccupied or there is no activity in the building. Keep windows and doors closed when bears may be in the area, especially at night. A secure house is your primary solution, but attractive odors must also be minimized. Occupancy is a major deterrent for most bears. If the residence will be vacant for periods of time, use heavily constructed, snug-fitting shutters on the windows and doors. A bear-resistant fence (chain-link or electric) surrounding your residence will keep most bears away from the house, as well as solve porch, patio and yard problems. Taped sounds, such as voices, dogs barking, gunshots, and explosions will deter bears. Dogs confined in a yard or tethered near the house are an excellent system to warn of a bear's presence, and will cause some bears to leave the area.

Move around buildings slowly, looking first and making adequate noise so as not to surprise a bear. Your residential area should be well lighted, but use a flashlight at night.

Foods

Foods of all types are the most odorous and sought-after attractants. Human foods are of higher quality—more easily digested, with more nutritional value—than a bear's natural food. Bears seek *all* human foods—fresh, packaged, frozen, canned, candy, gum, and bottled and canned drinks. Food scraps and crumbs on the floor, some hardly visible to a person, are *always* found whenever there is food, and are readily smelled by bears.

TO OUTWIT: Keep foods in tightly sealed containers and stored in closed cupboards and drawers. Keep floors, shelves, cabinets, appliances, and counters clean of food particles and spillage.

Food-Preparation Odors

The process of cooking food gives off odors and puts food vapors into the air that are blown to the outdoors through open windows and kitchen exhaust fans. Cooking smells drift with the wind for great distances, and are easily detected by bears. Food preparation ranks near the top of the attractant list.

TO OUTWIT: If bears have been frequenting the area, you may wish to prepare less odorous foods. Keep your windows and doors closed during food preparation and clean up immediately afterwards. Cleanliness is paramount.

Household Garbage and Trash

Garbage is the most common individual attractant and cause of conflicts between bears and people. Garbage is simply human food in a different form, often more smelly because it is unwrapped and in the process of decomposition. Garbage is something you would rather not keep in the house, and so it is ordinarily placed outside, where it becomes an easily available attractant. Your "dry" trash that has previously contained food—cereal boxes, cardboard cartons, wrappers, pop cans, plastic bottles, and paper—may seem quite "clean" to you, but it, too, has odors that attract bears.

TO OUTWIT: You should not burn your garbage and trash. This is *not* a solution. The "burn barrel" and trash-burner become major bear attractants. A household normally has a larger quantity of wet garbage than dry trash, and the ratio between the two does not permit complete incineration and the removal of odors. Use incineration for the disposal of garbage only if you have a commercial-type, gas-fired incinerator that *totally* incinerates wet garbage.

Do not bury your garbage. Bears easily detect it, and will quickly retrieve and scatter it over at least an acre.

Keep any fish or meat remains for disposal in your freezer or another cool, secure area until garbage disposal day. Place grease in a collection container with a lid (empty coffee can) and deposit it with garbage on disposal day.

Use sturdy plastic bags with ties for all garbage and trash—wet and dry. Do not place garbage outside the back door, even temporarily. Store all garbage that is inside your residence in cans with airtight lids. Use plastic bags to line the garbage cans.

Rinse bottles and cans before disposal (hopefully recycling). Store bottles and cans in a secure area such as a garage or outbuilding, and keep the doors and windows tightly closed. Avoid spillage—keep the storage areas spotless of scraps, leaking liquids, and trash on floors.

Clean all trash cans and storage areas regularly with hot water and bleach, ammonia, or lime to minimize residual odors. Do not place garbage outside if a storage area is full. Have bear-proof lids on any cans that must be outside.

Remember that the proper handling of garbage is difficult for small children.

In many locations, bear-proof bins such as Dumpsters are available from the disposal company. Sharing a large bin with neighbors is sometimes efficient. If you use these large storage containers, be certain they are big enough, so there is no overflow. Stabilize bins to keep bears from tipping them over. Keep them secure, bolting and locking

Garbage Scattered from Non-Bearproof Dumpsters   *Gary Brown*

Unprotected Garbage Scattered by a Bear   *Gary Brown*

all doors if necessary. Clean bins regularly as you would your garbage cans.

Animal-proof trash containers are commercially available. If storage buildings, Dumpsters, or other large containers are unavailable, use a chain-link fence enclosure with a top, an electric fence, or a combination of the two. Some people have a storage building for their garbage cans, and add an electric fence around it for additional security. Keeping dogs near garbage-storage areas, and keeping the areas well lit, will deter most bears. Protect your garbage from other animals, including birds that will scatter and make it available to bears.

If you have municipal or private trash pickup, make arrangements whereby your garbage is picked up without creating additional attractants. A garbage-pickup company in bear country should be very cognizant of the proper procedures. Watch out for garbage trucks that have liquids from compacted garbage leaking onto your driveway or in front of the house. Do not leave garbage out for an extended period of time. If you don't have commercial or municipal pickup, haul garbage and trash to an approved, bear-resistant disposal site as often as possible, but at least once a week to prevent odor buildup or overflow.

Cosmetics, Soaps, Cleansers, Medicines, and Plastics

Many areas within a residence have a variety of non-food items that attract bears. Medicines, cough syrups, candles, soaps, cosmetics, perfumes, toothpaste, cleansers, and film canisters are only a few that would be of little reward, to a bear, but are none the less attractive.

TO OUTWIT: Prevent spillage, keep containers clean, and store them in closed cabinets or drawers. Rely on your first line of defense—maintaining a secure residence and not attracting a bear to the area by having outside attractants.

Porches, Patios, and Yards

We eat, drink, play, and relax in our yard and on porches and patios. These areas are extensions of our house, and have similar bear attractants, such as food, garbage, vinyls, and pet food. Outside areas also tempt bears with bird feeders, flowers, vegetable gardens, and barbecues.

TO OUTWIT: A simple solution for these areas is to have a fence around the yard. Chain-link and other wire fences, at least eight feet high and buried two feet in the ground, are expensive, but effective. An electric fence is inexpensive and effective, but is only bear-resistant.

Keep your yard well lighted at night. Have bright yard lights that illuminate all areas—residence, garage, driveways, outbuildings, parking areas, yards, and patios. Well-lighted areas not only discourage some bears, but provide general security as well. Keep the areas around your residence and yard open, clear of dense vegetation, and free of natural bear foods. Yards surrounded by dense forests and high vegetation are more likely to have bear problems.

Again, cleanliness is paramount. Minimize food scraps on the ground and prevent spilled beverages. Clean and wipe down outdoor furniture and appliances that have been associated with foods. Hose down the areas of use when your activities are complete.

If a bear enters your yard to join an outdoor meal, very quickly remove all food, taking it indoors. Clean up the area if it is safe to do so.

Barbecue Grills and Accessories

Barbecue units, including grilling utensils, have highly attractive accumulations of grease, sauces, and food scraps. They also spread enticing odors. Liquid fire starter will also attract bears. Shortly after 1 A.M. on a summer night some thirty years ago, my wife and I were awakened by a loud crash, followed by a clanging of metal, on our back porch. We hurried to a window to determine the source of the disturbance. The noise was the destruction of the family barbecue, not recently cleaned, by a large grizzly bear that was standing on and attempting to extract itself from, a pile of twisted metal and scattered charcoal briquettes. The bear fled when it saw us at the window. Since then, we cleaned and stored our grill after each use.

TO OUTWIT: Use a propane or gas grill, and store it inside your garage or another secure building. Ceramic or stone briquettes should be burned off frequently to clean them. Allow the fire to go out or the briquettes to cool before storing a barbecue in a building. Clean your barbecue regularly and thoroughly, preferably after each use. While using the grill, locate it in an open area on the active side of the residence, and away from cover where bears might secretly approach.

Meat, Fish, and Fowl Smokers

Smokers are normally small, barbecue-size units, though larger smokehouses are used by people who put up hundreds of pounds of smoked fish, hogs, turkeys, and other meats each fall. All smokers will attract bears because of the odors they produce. The nature of the smoking process distributes a large volume of smoke and attractive odors. There is often a drainage of oils and meat juices onto the ground and floor.

TO OUTWIT: The best solution is not to have a smoker in bear country. However, if you must, then take precautions. Treat small, barbecue-size smokers as you would your barbecue grill. Smoke during daylight hours, and do not leave the smoker outside overnight. Clean up around the smoker area. Smokehouses should be strong and secure buildings that bears cannot enter. This is quite difficult, considering the venting and air exchange necessary for smoking. Electric fences, extra lighting, taped noises, and dogs will discourage bears from these facilities.

Food Lockers, Freezers, and Ice Chests

Any food-storage unit smells good to bears, even if empty. Some residences have inadequate indoor space for freezers and second refrigerators, or have outside food-storage lockers. These appliances are often kept on porches or in sheds and other buildings where they are available to bears. Ice chests, prime attractants, are often left available to bears. Some bears have learned to recognize ice chests as sources of food by sight alone.

The resident of a one-room cabin in Denali National Park had little inside space and kept his refrigerator on the front porch. One evening he heard a noise outside his door that sounded like his refrigerator being dragged across the porch. Opening the door, he faced a large grizzly bear not more than four feet away, standing with its forelegs and paws wrapped around the refrigerator, as if it was carrying off this newly claimed source of food. The resident slammed the substantial door, but the bear instantly smashed it into the cabin. The bear was standing at the threshold of the only door, and looking in. The resident turned and dove over a table, not touching a single item on the tabletop, and through closed French windows. Landing on the ground outside in a pile of window frames and glass, he quickly ran to a nearby house, where his lacerations were treated; he was later taken to a hospital for additional treatment. The bear came to the front door of the second house, stood up, pounded on and clawed the door, and peered through the door window at the victim and first aiders. The bear was chased away by loud shouting. There was no further damage to the individual's residence, the refrigerator was intact, and the bear was gone. But two nights later the bear returned to the house, attempted to gain entry, and was subsequently killed. The bear's history included receiving food rewards from other nearby residents and a hunting camp—it was food-conditioned and habituated to people.

TO OUTWIT: Keep food-storage appliances in your house if at all possible. If storage in a bear-resistant garage or outbuilding is necessary, keep the areas around the appliances clean of foods, and the building's windows and doors closed at all times.

Bird Feeders

Those who live in bear country enjoy the wildness of the area and all of its creatures, including birds. Feeders attract birds for our benefit only—the enjoyment of observing, photographing, and studying them. The birds do not need the food, summer or winter, spring or fall. They will survive without our supplementary feeding program.

Bird foods—especially sunflower seeds, suet, peanut butter, and the liquid food mixtures for hummingbirds—are bear attractants. In Massachusetts, from July 1997 to July 1999, there were 242 bear-damage complaints, of which 43 percent involved bird feeders.

Seed feeders normally have a substantial accumulation of bird feed on the ground under the feeder, which will attract bears and other animals such as skunks, opossums, and raccoons. As the seed accumulates on the ground, it rots and creates a more detectable attractant. Suet is also quite odorous, particularly during warm weather.

TO OUTWIT: Consider not feeding birds if you live in bear country, especially when natural bear foods are in short supply. If you do have feeders, locate them in areas where a bear would have to cross open space. Hang the feeders high—at least ten feet above ground—on a wire between trees, where they can be raised and lowered by a pulley system. Use seed trays or spill pans to prevent accumulation of seed on the ground. A simple electric fence around the feeder area or trees has been quite successful in deterring bears. Do not place feeders on porches or decks, and store them inside at night, feeding only during daylight hours. Feed suet only in the winter, when bears hibernate. Some bears have learned that feeders are available during the day, and have adjusted their feeding habits. In this case, hanging the feeders or fencing them in is absolutely necessary.

Another measure to outwit bears is to feed birds only during the hibernation period, which is December 1 through March 31 in most areas. Consult with your local wildlife-management agency for more specific dates.

Some people outwit bears by not feeding birds, but by providing bird houses, bird baths, and nesting materials to attract this cheerful, colorful, and interesting wildlife. Your local agricultural extension agent or wildlife agency can assist you in finding the shrubs and trees that attract birds, but not bears.

Swimming Pools and Hot Tubs

Bears have long been visitors to hot springs and private pools, but in the last ten to fifteen years, as more people have built homes with pools in bear country, the frequency of visits has increased. Any foods, drinks, garbage, and pool-cleaning chemicals left at a pool or hot tub will attract bears. Hot-tub covers—vinyl and foam materials— have attracted bears. Sometimes, bears are attracted to a pool as a body of water where they may drink, soak, cool off, or just swim and play. Bears frequenting a pool are close to people, creating the potential for a conflict.

TO OUTWIT: Keep the area clean. Always remove foods and garbage from the area. Store cleaning materials and chemicals inside a secure building. Have the area well lighted at night. A fenced yard (chain-link or electric), or just the pool fence (chain-link), will keep bears from frequenting the pool area. Watch your children—for obvious reasons, other than just conflicts with bears.

Children's Play Areas

Children have forts, play sets, tree houses, sandboxes, the yard, and many other outdoor areas for their activities.

Snacks are important elements in children's activities, and are often found in areas of play. Bear attractants accumulate as food scraps are dropped and drinks spilled.

Children move quickly, talking and shouting with high-pitched sounds. Youngsters are the size of bears' natural prey. These movements and noises are all stimuli that may provide signals for the predatory mode of a nearby bear.

On two occasions, I have observed a bear walk into a school playground while the children were in the class-room, and strike, paw, smell and "play" with playground equipment. The bear could have been attracted by the odor of synthetic materials or food scraps, or maybe it was simply mischievous. The incidents could as easily have occurred in a play area of a residence. One of these incidents is described under "Schools," later in this chapter.

TO OUTWIT: Have play areas in the open, close to the house. Keep your children in sight, and be able to reach them quickly. Teach and remind them about bears, and the precautions necessary when living in bear country. Provide foods and snacks in the house or on the porch or patio; keep foods out of the play areas. Have children in the house before dusk, and inside until after dawn, unless they are very closely supervised.

Children should play in the open, not in heavy, dense brush and shrubs. Teach them not to run around buildings or along trails, or to make animal sounds. They should never approach, pet, or feed any wild animal; any unknown dog or cat should be treated the same. If chil-

dren observe a bear, or any other wild or unfamiliar domestic animal, they should call for help.

Many years ago, my wife and I were in the front
room of our home, while our two daughters played
outside in a sparsely wooded area with three or four
other children. We could hear them laughing,
yelling and making the sounds expected of children
having fun. We looked out on them frequently. Suddenly, the children's sounds changed to frightened
screams, and we observed them scattering from their
area of play. Bolting out the door, we heard some of
the group yelling "bear." There was a young, relatively small, black bear walking into their midst as
they fled in several directions. However, our screaming four year old was not running. The cuff of one
pant leg was hooked on a branch stub of a log, and
she was frantically attempting to free herself as the
bear walked directly at her. Our nine year old was attempting to help her sister as I ran to the scene and
we lifted her free of the log. The bear had stopped
moving as I approached, but now walked up to
within eight inches of me. I chased the bear off and
it was subsequently removed from the area by bear
management authorities. We had failed to outwit
this bear, and have never been certain as to its intent
in approaching the group of children.

Pets

Most people have pets of one type or another. Pets that stay indoors rarely attract bears, but outdoor pets can. Many dogs spend most if not all of their time outside, and bears may be attracted to them as a food or because they are noisy pests. But the greatest and most common attractant associated with pets is their food. A park ranger in Alaska reported, "In a remote area of Alaska, a bear broke into a storage shed where 450 pounds of dog food were stored for sled dogs. The entire supply was consumed, with only slightly less than that many pounds deposited a few feet away on the porch in the form of bear scat."

Bears have harassed, preyed upon, and killed dogs, even attacking them on porches. Usually, human or pet food is what first attracts the bear. Then the dog becomes involved, triggering aggression by the bear. Small pets such as guinea pigs and rabbits, and their foods, will definitely attract bears.

TO OUTWIT: Store all pet foods in the house, garage, or other bear-resistant structures. If you must feed pets outside, do so during daylight hours, bring the bowls inside immediately after feeding, and clean up any spills and scraps. Enjoy small animals as indoor pets.

Kennel facilities in bear country have basically the same problems as residences with house and yard pets. Although the kennels have more pets and stored foods, they normally maintain tighter control of the animals and their foods. Still, precautions should be observed. (Refer to "Dogs" in chapter 5.)

Gardens

Many homes have vegetable and flower gardens, some large, most small. The problem here is quite simple—vegetable gardens provide quantities of attractive and nourishing foods for bears. These plants are readily available and similar to the foods bears struggle to find in the wild. One gardener, who was proud of his carrot crop, found bear tracks in his garden one morning. His lengthy carrot rows were still there, but the carrot tops were all lying neatly to one side of the excavated rows, and the carrots were missing. Tracks indicated a grizzly bear had deftly dug up the carrots with its long claws, and consumed the nourishing tuber portion of the plants, leaving the uninteresting tops.

TO OUTWIT: Vegetable gardening in occupied bear habitat is not the best idea, but it can be accomplished with a few precautions. Consider crops that will not attract bears; consult with your local wildlife management agency or agricultural extension service for guidance. Plant gardens in open areas, away from shrubs, brush and forested areas, and enclose them with electric fences. Try a scarecrow (fun for the kids to build), but change its location frequently. Carefully maintain the garden, keeping it clean of rotting vegetation and produce, and harvest your produce as soon as it is ripe to lessen the period of attraction. Store containers of commercial fertilizers in a secure building.

The taking of flowers and digging up of flower gardens by bears appears to be opportunistic, and a minimal problem, but the situation is difficult to solve. Not planting flowers is out of the question. An electric fence is one solution, though it detracts from the beauty of your flowers. Many residents just live with a potential problem, which is not the best idea, or use a bear-proof fence around the entire yard.

Blueberries, raspberries, strawberries, and many others are delicious for jams and jellies, on cereals, in pies and cobblers, or just for snacks, but are all very attractive to bears. The crop is similar, if not identical, to natural berry patches. It's best not to plant berries in bear country. But if you do enjoy having a berry patch, use an electric fence to deter bears. Pick berries promptly as they ripen, and keep the patch clean, without rotting berries on the ground.

Compost Areas

Composing has become more common in recent years. Compost can be very odorous and quite attractive to bears as a food, especially if food scraps and other wet garbage are included in the process. Composting is contrary to the proper handling of garbage in bear country. Even piles of grass cuttings will attract bears.

TO OUTWIT: If you compost, consider a community effort by which many families are served and the process is conducted in a secure building, with minimal escape of odors, or in an area surrounded by an electric fence. Do not place meats, sweets, melon rinds, or fruits in your compost piles or containers. If your compost requirements are minimal, a small bucket in a secure area, such as your basement or under the kitchen sink, might serve your needs. Better yet, purchase your compost at the local nursery, supermarket, ranch-supply, or hardware store.

Greenhouses

Flower and vegetable greenhouses are basically the same as the outside gardens, except that there is more to lose if a bear forcibly enters the building, damaging the structure, the misting and fan systems, plant tables, and other equipment. The plant losses may be expensive if you are raising orchids, fuchsias, and other houseplants, or if the greenhouse is a large commercial operation.

TO OUTWIT: The most practical measure is to use an electric fence around a greenhouse, and then take all the precautions you would for an outdoor garden. Have the greenhouse in the open, away from dense vegetation that provides cover for bears. Dogs may deter bears, and will warn you of a bear's presence.

Livestock

Many residents of bear country keep horses, ponies, llamas, burros, goats, sheep, pigs, cows, and smaller domestic
animals such as ducks, rabbits, pheasants, and chickens.
Husbanding livestock in bear country is not the best idea,
since the animals and their feeds are highly attractive to
bears. Bears have attacked and killed all sizes of domestic
animals, though the easier prey are calves, colts, pigs,
sheep, chickens, and animals confined in cages.

Livestock foods (grain, chicken feed, rabbit pellets,
horse cubes), some with molasses-type additives, are common attractants and have long been a serious problem in
bear country. Spilling and scattering livestock foods is
quite normal, and develops a readily available reward for
bears. There is often a large volume of stored feed associated with livestock.

Animals die, and livestock carcasses quickly become
very smelly and quite attractive to bears—not to mention
quite unpleasant for you. Saddles, bridles, and other tack,
all with an accumulation of oils and sweat, have attracted
bears. In one case, an individual spent two and a half days
searching for his saddle in a heavily wooded area before
he found it—in a very unusable condition.

TO OUTWIT: Preferably, you should not have pigs, goats,
and sheep. Keep your caged animals and smaller livestock
in a barn or other secure building at night, and keep
larger animals in at night if a bear is in the area. Store tack

in bear-resistant buildings, and handle garbage and trash the same as at your residence. Use electric fences around small fields, pastures, corrals, pens, and cages, and keep the areas well lighted at night.

Store all livestock foods in a bear-resistant building or container. There are large metal bear-proof storage containers commercially available. Use feeders that minimize spillage, and feed only the amount the animals will eat to prevent leftovers. Do not dispose of a carcass, regardless of size, on your property or in the area. Haul all carcasses to an approved landfill, or have them collected by a rendering plant, *immediately*. Small, rabbit-size carcasses should be sealed in plastic bags and disposed of with your household garbage. This may be quite difficult if the bunny is a favorite pet. In that case, ask your veterinarian for assistance.

Garages and Storage Buildings

A variety of bear attractants may be found in buildings other than your house. Foods in extra refrigerators and freezers, canned goods, dry foods, camping supplies, petroleum products, paints, chemicals, and recyclables are some of the attractants stored in garages, sheds, and other outbuildings. Many storage buildings are not resistant to any bear that is determined to reach an attractant inside. An embarrassed resort owner in Wyoming related this incident:

> I had about fifteen cases of food, eight cases of paper items, and several cans of garbage in my bear-

proof storage building. We had built the building with 2-by-4 studs, sixteen inches apart, and covered it with sheets of ¼-inch plywood, and a heavy tar-paper-type sheeting. We used ½-inch-thick rough-wood siding (six-inch-wide boards) on the outside and it was all nailed real well. That black bear removed most of the siding of one wall, then ripped out the plywood and two studs, and made a three-foot by five-foot hole through it all. The bear went in and out of the building and hauled the food and garbage outside where it ate all night. It also tore up most of the cases of paper things inside. That bear was big and could hardly run, it was so full when we came out in the morning.

Bears are attracted to the odors of petroleums, paints, and chemicals, as well as antifreeze, oil, fertilizers, transmission fluid, oily rags, solvents, oil filters, gasoline, concrete cleaner, lamp oil, plastics, vinyls, and other similar items. Bears don't necessarily consume these items, but will investigate and bite into the container, spilling its contents, creating a mess, and possibly ingesting harmful chemicals. A black bear in a Wyoming community was observed with bright orange color on its muzzle, with streaks radiating from its mouth back and up to its eyes and ears. The bear had obviously bitten into an aerosol can of spray paint. Another bear was observed tipping up an open, partially full can of motor oil, and drinking it like soda pop.

People commonly overlook recyclables as attractants. All food containers and packaging have residual odors even when rinsed for recycling deposit. Storage at home is sometimes a problem due to volume and the need to separate the various items.

TO OUTWIT: Store all foods, food-storage appliances, petroleum products, chemicals, paints, other similar products, and recyclables only in bear-resistant, heavily constructed buildings. Keep the buildings clean, and keep doors and windows closed at all times. Use tight-fitting window shutters and doors that bears cannot use their claws to pull open. Carports are obviously not secure and should be free of any attractants. Dispose of oily rags in airtight containers. Thoroughly wash recyclables and store them with the same security as garbage and trash. Haul them to a recycling center or depository at least once a week. Keep areas well lighted, and consider the use of electric fences around buildings. Again, dogs may help deter bears.

Preventing Conflicts on Ranches and Farms

Most ranchers, farmers, their families, and employees in bear country have contended with bears for many years. They have addressed and resolved problems with a variety of solutions. I hope these pages provide some new approaches and methods that will mean improved protection for people and their property, and better appreciation and preservation of bears.

Ranches and farms have much in common with individual residences. However, they are larger, more complex operations, and have greater amounts and numbers of almost everything—people, foods, garbage, livestock, residences, outbuildings, vehicles, garages, pets, and crops. The types of attractants are no different than those of an individual residence; they are simply multiplied.

Field Crops

Field crops such as corn, sugar cane and beets, sweet potatoes, melons, snap beans, berries, sunflowers, and numerous types of vegetables are highly inviting to bears. Grains such as wheat, barley, buckwheat, oats and others have attracted bears to croplands. Bears not only consume quantities of these nutritious foods, but inflict damage on the fields. They sample vegetables and trample grains as they investigate and feed, biting into melons, knocking down sunflowers, and leaving "crop circle" patterns in oat fields. Bears also break into silos and bins to get stored crops.

Farms that have fruit- and vegetable-packing operations usually have piles of culls that are notorious for attracting bears. They often have family vegetable gardens, too.

TO OUTWIT: Consider planting crops that will not attract bears. Otherwise, leave unplanted, mowed, open lanes between crops and forests and other dense vegetation. Alternate row crops to lessen cover for a bear, and plow under or otherwise clean up excess crops. Inspect fields frequently to detect and correct problem situations. Harvest crops as quickly as possible, and dispose of culls at sanitary landfills or bury them immediately in an isolated ranch dump. Use electric fences where feasible. Some farmers have used dogs to chase bears away from crops. Store fertilizers in bear-resistant buildings or containers.

Fruit and Nut Orchards

Farms across Canada and the United States have thousands of acres of fruits and nuts—apples, pears, plums, oranges, cherries, pomegranates, peaches, walnuts, almonds, tungnuts, pecans, and similar crops. Bears seek out these highly nutritious foods and nuts when they are ripe, standing on their hind legs and pulling down branches to reach the fruit. If the trees are strong enough, the bears will climb into them to reach higher branches and strip fruit. Besides losing the crops to bears, farmers also suffer damage to or the loss of trees. Bears are attracted to all orchards, but they seem to have a special fondness for fruit that has fallen to the ground and is rotting.

Bears are also attracted to vineyards by ripening grapes, and to sugar-maple groves during the sap harvest. Grapes and sap are lost, and vines and trees are damaged.

TO OUTWIT: You are undoubtedly better off if you do not have orchards where bears abound, but, ironically, the best growing conditions for certain crops happen to be in bear country. Electric fences have been quite successful in protecting many orchards. But the attractant remains. Timely harvesting minimizes the period of attraction. Prompt removal of fallen fruits prevents the even more aromatic attraction of fruits rotting on the ground.

Livestock

Adult cattle are seldom taken by bears, except for a rare kill by a black bear and occasional kills in brown-bear country. Calves are of course more easily taken, and calving afterbirth is often an attractant. Horses have been attacked, but actual deaths are more fable than fact. Many ranchers say they sustain far more livestock losses from two-legged predators than from any other cause.

While all livestock are attractants, hogs, sheep, goats, chickens, ducks, geese, and other small creatures seem particularly popular with bears, maybe because they are easier to take. Hogs are difficult for bears to catch if not tightly corralled. Many rabbit hutches and chicken coops have been demolished as bears sought these smaller animals and their foods. Poultry farms are vulnerable to losses due to the number and confinement of chickens and turkeys.

Sheep are in greater jeopardy than other livestock, and must be closely herded. Besides directly killing them, bears have frightened and "stampeded" sheep into fence corners where large numbers die from crushing and suffocation. According to Herrero, in *Bear Attacks,* "The record for sheep kills by a single bear in one attack probably goes to a black bear in Idaho that killed 235 sheep by running them off a cliff during the summer of 1980."

State of Montana Game Warden (retired), and bear and lion trapper, Dave Wedum tells this story of a rancher/bear conflict:

> Several years ago, a rancher west of Kalispell, Montana contacted him claiming his pigs were starving because of bears. The rancher would summon his pigs—fifteen to twenty—with the traditional hog call of "suoiee," and within a few minutes, two small, two-year-old black bears would arrive, enter his pig pen and eat the "slop"—the pigs' food—acting as if they could not care less about the pigs. Once the bears had their fill, they would leave and the rancher would feed more slop to the pigs. The pigs were not truly starving, but they were getting less food than necessary, and their owner was worried that as time went on, he would not have adequate food for them. Warden Wedum trapped and relocated the bears, and there was no further competition for the slop—except between the pigs.

TO OUTWIT: Some ranches forego small livestock altogether. If you do keep food and small animals, use intensive herding—avoid pasturing animals in isolated areas, near heavy cover and streams, or where bear travel corridors exist, and move livestock into protected areas if a bear is in the area. Contain animals near or in barns and stables at night, and have the areas well lighted. Electric fences for small pastures, pens, corrals, feed bins, sick pens, and calving areas are highly effective. Trained guard dogs for cattle are used by some ranchers.

Birthing of animals should occur at the barn or other protected building. If field birthing is necessary, remove afterbirth, which quickly attracts bears, coyotes, and foxes. Immediately remove all livestock carcasses from pastures and fields.

Feeds for cattle, mules, horses, swine, chickens, and rabbits are common attractants and a serious problem in bear country. Feed in open areas if possible, but close to the ranch buildings. Use timed and controlled feeding mechanisms that hang well above the ground, minimize spillage, and deliver feed at a rate that avoids creating left-overs available to bears. Feeding bins should not be scattered, and there should be specific feeding sites where any spillage is confined to small areas. Store all livestock foods in bear-resistant buildings if possible, and use electric fences around large outside storage areas.

Livestock Carcasses

Dead livestock means an economic loss. The other, more immediate problem is the disposal of a large carcass that will rapidly become a bear attractant.

TO OUTWIT: Promptly attend to any carcass. Do not dispose of a carcass in a ranch or farm dump unless it can receive a deep and prompt burial, and only then if this disposal measure is known to be successful in your area. Burn combustibles over the top of the burial. It's better to haul a carcass to an approved sanitary landfill or have a rendering plant immediately collect it.

In some areas, the recommended disposal method is to scatter carcasses so that bears may scavenge them, but without creating a depository where bears expect a continual source of food. Seek the guidance of your wildlife-management agency.

Garbage Dumps

Ranch and farm dumps receive an incredible assortment of items: metals, carcasses, wood and paper products, tree cuttings, fruits and vegetables, household garbage, and dairy and livestock garbage. Vegetable and fruit culls are sometimes disposed of by the hundreds of pounds, creating an aromatic attractant, especially as the produce rots. Livestock carcasses and slaughterhouse or poultry-processing residues placed in dumps will quickly become highly odorous attractants.

TO OUTWIT: Locate your dump in a very remote area of the ranch or farm, well away from your homesite, neighbors' homes, and operations. Have a piece of equipment available to immediately bury anything that will not burn.

Burn the dump whenever you deposit combustible materials, using an accelerant to facilitate a hot and complete burn that will minimize odors. Burying does not totally eliminate smells.

Use an electric fence (welded-wire type) around the dump. This is an ideal situation for a solar panel unit.

If you are unable to prevent attracting bears to your dump, haul or have hauled all food, garbage, carcasses and other bear attractants to an approved sanitary landfill. Burn the remainder of your trash.

Water Troughs, Ponds, and Salt Blocks (Licks)

Bears use livestock water troughs and ponds for their intended purpose—a convenient source of drinking water. Salt blocks are an attractive source of minerals.

I have observed a large black bear, 250 to 300 pounds, with its front paws on the edge of a livestock trough, and its snout in the water, drinking. There were no livestock in the immediate area, and the bear, ignoring the nearby people, drank for approximately two minutes before walking away into the trees.

A bear attracted to these water and mineral sources may discourage livestock from using them, or, even worse, ambush an animal, most likely a calf or colt. One bear pulled off and damaged a trough float, draining the water tank. Another bear stole—simply carried off—a fifty-pound block of salt.

TO OUTWIT: There should be no serious bear conflicts if troughs, ponds, and sources of salt are well away from any buildings, corrals, or feeding areas. Monitor for bear sign and move livestock if a threat exists. Provide protective covers for water-trough floats and valves. Share the salt with the bears—the attractant is very short-term, and it is unlikely that too many blocks will be stolen. If a problem persists, aversive conditioning (rubber bullets) by you or a wildlife agency may be necessary.

Apiaries (Beehives)

Seventeenth-century writer Edward Topsell, in *The History of Four-Footed Beasts* (1607) wrote, ". . . and [bears] will break into Bee-hives sucking out the Hony." Bears' interest in beehives has not changed since the 1600s. Loss of bees, larvae, and honey, plus the damage to hives and other apiary equipment, is the most costly agricultural problem caused by bears in North America. The bears are actually more interested in the brood (bee larvae) than the honey, but obviously do not pass up the sweetness of this food as they smash and completely destroy the hives.

As they collect larvae and honey, the bears are incessantly stung, and they whine and squeal as their eyes and ears are attacked and the bees burrow deep in their fur. But they are persistent and not at all deterred by the discomfort of stings.

TO OUTWIT: The best solution is to not keep bees in occupied bear habitat, but if you do, several measures can prevent losses and bear damage. Electric fences are the most successful means of protecting beehives. Ron Barnett, a beekeeper in southwestern Montana for forty years, enthusiastically describes his success using electric fences.

We had severe losses from bears, thousands of dollars, but haven't had a problem since we designed the electric fence of welded-wire [six-inch squares] panels with three electric tapes [wires], to enclose the hives. The panels are fifty-two inches high and eight feet long, and the three electric tapes are on six-inch extensions around the panels. The tapes are

Gary Brown

Beehives with Bees and Honey Protected from Bears by an Electric Fence   *Gary Brown*

six inches above the ground, midway up the welded wire and at the top of the panels, and we use solar-panel energizers to power the fence.

One large black bear sat on its haunches in front of the fence, and put its paws up to within an inch of the tapes, turned its head from side to side, acted as if it could sense the charge, or maybe it could hear the "snap" of the electric charge from the energizer. It then put its nose up to the tape once, then again, pushing it into the wire panel. That was enough. Hit with the electric charge, it ran off shaking its head, and then climbed a tree. The system works well, in all weather, and is good for homes, yards, rustic cabins, many places. We haven't had a problem.

In addition to using electric fences, group your hives or apiaries, consolidating them into the smallest area that can be practically managed, and maintain cleared, mowed corridors around them. Place your hives as far from dense vegetation as possible, and away from streams; agricultural agents recommend at least fifty yards. Some beekeepers place their hives on rooftops or on bear-resistant elevated platforms with metal poles, and others use sturdy railroad-tie structures. Harvest the honey as soon as possible to lessen the period of attraction. Aversive conditioning (plastic bullets, loud sounds) is an option with a bear that continues to return to the area. Consult your local fish-and-game department or agricultural agent for recommendations.

Vehicles and Roads

Recreational Vehicles

Recreational vehicles are normally parked outside, and usually contain foods and other attractants similar to those in your home. The structure of these vehicles is *not* bear-resistant. They are readily broken into by bears.

TO OUTWIT: If you are unable to store your RV in a bear-resistant building, treat it the same as your house. Keep the doors, windows, and vents closed, and keep the interior extremely clean. If you must park it outside for more than a few days, or if a bear is frequenting the area, remove foods and other attractants, and tether a dog nearby. Better yet, use a simple electric fence, and maybe a dog as well. Keep your parking areas well lighted.

Automobiles, Sport-Utility Vehicles, and Pickups

An automobile, pickup, or sport-utility vehicle without a bear attractant somewhere inside would be an extreme rarity. Foods, cosmetics, medicines, gum and candy wrappers, beverages, the remnant smell of groceries, a roll of antacid wafers, a half-eaten sandwich, cookie crumbs, and dog food are only a few examples of items normally found in vehicles. All will attract bears.

Bears will enter a vehicle through an open window, but are also quite capable of gaining entry by breaking windows, and even by grabbing the top of a car door and bending the door to a ninety-degree angle. As for convertibles—need more be said?

Neighbors, a quarter-mile from my home, parked a sedan in front of their residence, following a take-out meal from a McDonalds. They left beverage cups, food wrappers and containers, certainly some scraps and crumbs, and a quantity of french fries in the front seat of the vehicle. During the night, a black-bear sow with two cubs was attracted to the car. She hooked her claws on the top of the door window, which was open approximately one inch, and easily pulled out and shattered the window. Climbing into the car, she collected the reward for herself and the cubs.

Gary Brown

Car Door Pulled Down by a Black Bear Seeking Food Attractants in the Vehicle Trunk
Gary Brown

Upon entering a vehicle, a bear might tear out the back seat, gaining access to food in the trunk. Most vehicles are constructed so that entry from the interior to the trunk is impossible, but by the time the bear is thwarted, the back seat and most of the car's interior is destroyed. A bear in the front seat of your vehicle, pursuing an attractant in your glove compartment, will probably obtain the item with a delicate touch that removes the dashboard. And bears have been known, not infrequently, to defecate and urinate while in a vehicle.

Several years ago, a newspaper article described an interesting encounter in Alaska. As a young man approached his car, he found a black bear investigating the driver's-side door. To avoid the bear, he quickly jumped into the front seat by way of the passenger-side door, only to find that another bear had already gained entry through an open window and was in the back seat. Not wanting to share the vehicle with a bear, he quickly exited, leaving the bears to rummage through the car.

TO OUTWIT: When a vehicle is not in use, keep it free of all foods and other attractants, including food containers and wrappers, medicines, gum, pet foods, groceries, and snacks. Maintain a clean vehicle, promptly cleaning up any spills. Park vehicles indoors if possible, but always keep windows and doors tightly closed.

Snowmobiles and All-Terrain Vehicles

Lunches, snacks, and other attractants are frequently in the storage compartments of these vehicles. Their seats are composed of vinyl coverings that, when warmed by the sun, emit fumes that have attracted bears. Fuel spilled on the seats provides an added attractant. The vehicles are most often parked outside, available to bears.

A radio technician was returning from a mountain-top radio repeater in Wyoming during the spring. He was traveling on a snowpacked mountain trail when his machine had mechanical problems. He hiked out to obtain a new engine belt, leaving his machine overnight. On his return the next morning, he began finding pieces of vinyl seat cover and seat padding more than 200 yards before he reached his snowmobile. The evidence indicated that a bear had been attracted to the machine, or happened upon it, and tore out the gasoline-scented vinyl seat.

TO OUTWIT: Remove all foods, drinks, snacks, lotions, lubricants, and other potential attractants from the storage areas of these vehicles. Use caution to prevent fuel spills on the machines. Park the vehicle in a bear-resistant building if possible.

Boats and Boat Houses

Some residents of bear country live on lake shores or along rivers, and have boats for transportation and recreational purposes. Boats often have the same attractants as vehicles: foods, beverages, suntan lotions, and garbage. When bears are attracted to boats, the resulting damage is predictable: storage compartments torn open, seats, cushions, life preservers, and vinyl tops ripped and destroyed. Boat gunwales and outboard motor fuel lines have been chewed and damaged. Boat houses are rarely bear resistant, and often contain attractants. Remember that bears are excellent swimmers; moored boats may be vulnerable to investigation and damage.

TO OUTWIT: Keep boats clean. Remove all attractants from boats and boat houses when not in use. Store life preservers, cushions, and fuel supplies in secure cabinets or other facilities.

Roadsides

Need I describe the amount of garbage, trash, and other debris along our roads and highways? Any roadside garbage or other attractant may draw bears into the areas where you reside, providing the opportunity for them to investigate your residence and activities. Also, bears are struck and killed by vehicles as they cross the road near an attractant.

TO OUTWIT: If you don't have a volunteer highway-cleanup program in your area, contact your local maintenance department and wildlife agency to promote such an effort, or at least to have them remove the roadside bear attractants.

Roadkill

A variety of animals are struck and killed by vehicles along our roads and highways. As roadkills decompose, odors increase enough for bears to detect this source of food from great distances. Although they may be attracted to nearby residences where conflicts may occur, a more common problem is the bear becoming a roadkill as it is struck by a vehicle. The result is a damaged vehicle, injury to the vehicle occupants, and a dead bear—a roadkill to attract more bears.

TO OUTWIT: Your local road department should promptly remove roadkills, depositing them in approved sanitary landfills. You should report roadkills near your home to the appropriate office. If these bear attractants are allowed to remain along your roads, take action—contact highway departments, wildlife-management offices, or other agencies to urge an improvement in the removal process.

Places Where Children Gather

Schools

The normal activities at a large school usually deter bears from the area during the day. Smaller, more isolated schools might have bears enter the school grounds during daylight hours, and bears may prowl and investigate any school at night.

Bears are attracted to school food facilities, playground areas, and vehicles. Attractants exist primarily in the form of foods and garbage, though there are many other items similar to those in residential situations. Several years ago, I observed an adult black bear walk onto the school playground in Yosemite Valley (the children were in their classrooms). It went directly to the playground equipment and began investigating—cautiously sniffing—the equipment and the area in general. The bear swatted a swing seat, and seemed momentarily startled by the rattle of the hanging chains, but continued striking the seat, knocking it about three feet into the air. Next, it stood on its hind legs, smelled the hanging pull-up bar for a few seconds, then swatted the bar two or three times, until the bar swung back and struck the bear in the side of the head. Dropping to all four legs, the bear hit the swing seat again and bounded away, across a meadow and into the forest. There was definitely curiosity involved in the bear's behavior. Most likely it was attracted to the odors of equipment materials, people, and possibly food, but I felt there was a bit of mischievousness as well in all of its actions, especially that "one last punch."

TO OUTWIT: Snacks and other foods should be confined to indoors. Cafeteria sanitation and appropriate handling of food and garbage is highly important in preventing the attraction of bears. Always supervise small children when they are outside. If a bear is in the area, bring them inside immediately. (Refer to "Children's Play Areas" and "Residences" earlier in this chapter.)

Summer Camps

Camps have the same problems as a residence, but with a larger number of people, usually young, most of whom have not lived in bear country and have no idea of the necessary precautions. And, there are mess halls with much greater quantities of food, and the old nemesis—attractive garbage. Some camps have horses for riding activities. An Alaska resident's report to the Alaska Department of Fish and Game, from Larry Kaniut's *Alaska Bear Tales,* describes a mess hall problem:

> . . . [T]he bear had torn siding off the outside wall to gain entry, creating a hole roughly two feet square. Inside the bear had consumed or destroyed one case of bread, one crate of cabbage, one sack of onions, and one-third crate of peaches. . . . [During two previous break-ins] windows were broken, an outside door was broken down, and the bear ate or destroyed twenty-five dozen eggs, five quarts of milk, and one-half case each of apples, cantaloupes and oranges.

Any such incident can make for frightened and hungry youngsters.

TO OUTWIT: Preventive measures are basically the same as those at residences and their associated areas. Camp authorities must provide detailed instruction to the camp participants regarding living in bear country, followed up by close monitoring and supervision.

Any camp should have bear-resistant food-storage areas, and excellent sanitation in the food-handling areas. It should also have bear-resistant garbage cans and bins, with daily removal to a sanitary landfill.

Community Facilities

Sewage-Disposal Plants, Sanitary Landfills (Dumps)

There is an extensive history of bears being attracted and rewarded with garbage from dumps, items from sewage lagoons, and dried sludge from disposal plants. Sanitary landfills have in the past been one of the greatest attractants of bears. For many people, it was a pastime to visit a dump and watch bears forage for "food," but in most areas this is no longer possible, as fences and other appropriate management have eliminated bears from landfills. But where bears are attracted to these facilities, they will definitely visit nearby residences, lodges, and ranches. Dump bears are the true "problem" bears.

TO OUTWIT: The elimination of bear attractants is virtually impossible, but bears can be denied rewards. The managers of disposal areas have responsibilities to operate them so that bears cannot obtain rewards. The facilities should be fenced. Garbage in landfills must be promptly buried—daily if at all possible. If bears are attracted to the area, and remain even without rewards, your wildlife-management agency should consider aversive conditioning or other measures to remove the bears. Contact the appropriate sanitation or wildlife agencies.

Public Parks and Campgrounds

Picnics in the park and camping produce an abundance of odors, scraps, and garbage. Bears are attracted not only to parks and campgrounds, but also to nearby residences, businesses, and other facilities. Many campers and picnickers unwittingly food-condition bears.

TO OUTWIT: Parks and campgrounds must have bear-resistant garbage cans or Dumpsters, appropriate garbage pickup, firepit cleanup, and good general maintenance. Good information for visitors about camping and picnicking in bear country is essential. When bears frequent these areas, contact the agency responsible for parks and campgrounds and your wildlife-management agency, and request appropriate bear-management practices.

Natural Foods, Forest Fires, and Dens

Foods

Bears might enter your living space because of natural foods near your residence, maybe even in your yard. Such visits increase the opportunities for a conflict. Bears are more likely to show up at your residence during a poor natural-food year, or in the fall, when bears gorge themselves in preparation for hibernation.

Bears seek natural foods such as small animals, fish, crustaceans, bees and other insects, squirrel middens (food-storage mounds), acorns, hickory and beech nuts, berry patches, fruits from trees and shrubs, grasses, and corms and roots from a variety of plants. All of these necessities may be near your home. In some areas, particularly Alaska and Canada, spawning runs of salmon choke the streams with fish, providing an abundance of high-protein food. Bears congregate along these water courses, where some people have constructed homes.

TO OUTWIT: Utilize all of the previous measures applicable to your living situation. Do not give bears any reason to investigate your home and outbuildings. Living on a spawning stream in Alaska is not a good idea.

Fire Camps and Firelines

Wildfires are part of living in bear country. They can occur near any residence, and fire-suppression activities may be of the magnitude to require a fire camp. Fire camps are a source of food and garbage. These temporary camps have few, if any, bear-proof buildings. The highest priority in these camps is the fire; little thought is given to bears and the attractants that will cause conflicts. This problem has improved considerably during the past few years, but still exists in many fire situations where large quantities of foods and garbage are often stored in tents or out in the open. Bears are attracted to camps, where they receive rewards, damage property, and create havoc.

Firefighters carry meals with them along the firelines, and on some occasions fireline camps may be established.

Food storage and garbage disposal along firelines have improved, though trash and garbage are still thrown into the fire and littered along the firelines. Bears that receive food rewards in fire camps are obviously willing to be near people. The result is bears conditioned to human foods and habituated to people. Your residence is the next step when the firefighters and their foods are gone.

TO OUTWIT: During a fire in your neighborhood, you probably have more to consider than bear attractants. If you can, contact the firefighters and your local wildlife-management agency to remind them of the problem of bear attractants and the long-term ramifications. If you must evacuate because of the threat of fire, be sure to have everything secured from bears.

Denning (Hibernation) Areas

Black bears might seek almost any cavity or opening for a den in which to hibernate. Occasionally, they come into areas of human occupancy, where they find an opening under a house, restaurant, or other building in which to spend the winter. A bear could establish a den under one of your buildings without your knowing. For two days during the late fall many years ago, I and others observed a female black bear prowling around several buildings, including a cafeteria, in Yellowstone National Park. The cafeteria had a two-foot crawl space beneath it, and a small door was missing. No one thought much about the bear when it was no longer visible in the area, *until* spring, when she emerged from under the cafeteria, with two new cubs. Fortunately, she did not remain in the area.

TO OUTWIT: Be aware of any potential denning sites at or near your home, ranch, or farm. Close any opening that might be used as a den. If bears are in your area in the late fall and early winter, have you local wildlife-management agency discourage any denning that will conflict with your normal winter and spring activities.

Intentionally Feeding Bears

Deliberately providing food for bears—baiting to attract bears for observation—is illegal in most jurisdictions. Intentionally feeding bears results in as many conflicts in some areas as does the availability of garbage, but causes more injuries than any other action or attractant.

Sam Stokes, Sr., a regional wildlife biologist in South Carolina, recently related, "We have had reports of some individuals who open their doors to bears so they can feed them inside their homes. This is a real powder-keg situation."

People feed bears at residences, restaurants, stores, lodges, and motels. Incredibly, a few hotels and lodges have been known to provide wakeup calls when a bear arrived for garbage and other foods set out at a "feeding" area.

If you feed bears, you make them food conditioned and habituated to people. You can put yourself and others in danger. When the provided food supply is gone, a bear often seeks more. Sure, you are safe at the moment, observing from a secure area, but that fed bear may become aggressive and eventually approach or attack, and inflict serious injury on someone. The act of feeding bears will come back to "bite you in the end," or another body part.

Paul Davidson, executive director of the Black Bear Conservation Committee in Baton Rouge, Louisiana, relates this bear feeding story:

An employee of an oil company pipeline facility in southern Louisiana summoned assistance from our organization, reporting that a bear had broken into their administration building over the weekend. The bear had gained entry by partially pulling a window frame out of the wall and entering through the opening, and then had opened their refrigerator, and made a "terrible mess." This bear had been in the area for about six weeks, but had not been a problem. Upon my arrival at their offices, I was shown a handful of Polaroid photographs of a bear on the conference-room table. I immediately believed the bear had broken into the building when everybody was at work, but was sheepishly advised that the photographs were taken a few days prior to the break-in, when "we put a chair in the back door [blocking it open] and dropped doughnuts down the hall to lead her to the table so we could take her picture."

The bear moved away within two weeks but showed up about six miles down the road three months later where she was finding food at Dumpsters and people were feeding her.

The oil-company staff was lucky that the bear did not become "threatened" while on the conference-room table and seriously injure one or several people. The bear had obviously "cased the joint" on her doughnut foray, had received a reward, knew this source of food, and knew exactly where to go for more, even though the chair was no longer holding open the back door. The good news, according to Davidson, is, "we moved her and she has had three litters of cubs since then and neither she nor her cubs have caused any problems."

TO OUTWIT: Plain and simple—**Do not feed the bears!**

Feeding other animals, such as raccoons, opossums, wild pigs, foxes, coyotes, feral dogs and cats, squirrels, and deer at your residence will attract bears and create serious problems. I waver on the question of feeding birds. If you must feed the birds, use the measures provided under "Bird Feeders," earlier in this chapter. Do not feed *any other* wildlife!

Living compatibly with bears is a goal worthy of pursuit. We should do our very best to minimize, if not totally prevent, conflicts with bears. Because bears are unpredictable, we should not be disheartened or give up if we have a failure.

A revision of President Abraham Lincoln's words perfectly describes our challenge:

> You may outwit all of the bears some of the time;
>
> You can even outwit some of the bears all of the time;
>
> But you can't outwit all of the bears all of the time.

If you fail to outwit a bear, further action on your part is necessary. Conflicts must be resolved, further conflicts prevented, or the bear might need to be expelled from the area.

Five

Resolving Conflicts

First, I hope that you apply all of the appropriate measures presented in chapter 4 and that they work. Those actions are proven to prevent conflicts between people and bears. But outwitting bears is an inexact science. You may have a lapse—forget to take in the bird feeders or secure a garbage can lid—overlook something, or find your measures inadequate for the situation. Perhaps a bear is drawn by other neighborhood attractants, or maybe there is no obvious explanation. For whatever reason, a bear arrives in your area. Getting it to leave can tax your ingenuity and willpower.

A story told by Dave Wedum, a retired Montana game warden and bear trapper, is an example of a bear that won the battle of wits, at least for a year. By 1975, numerous summer residences had been built near the North Fork of the Flathead River in northwest Montana. These "cabins" were strongly constructed buildings, with heavy, two-inch-thick window shutters. The doors were also heavily constructed and had strong hinges, latches, and bolts. The owners were people who conscientiously kept their cabins and adjacent areas clean, leaving nothing outside that might attract bears. Everything was normal for several years, until early that summer, when a 700- to 800-pound, twenty-year-old, male grizzly bear came into the picture. He broke into twenty-three of the summer residences, some two or three times. All of the break ins except one (the bear departed when it discovered the occupant) occurred while the cabins were unoccupied. He broke down the cabin doors, sometimes forcing the door casing and parts of the walls completely into a cabin. Once inside a cabin, the bear obtained food, damaging only areas where food was stored.

An all-out, multi-agency effort was mounted to remove this destructive bear. Some of the finest bear trappers in the western United States were involved. Traps were set— snares, jaw traps, and culvert traps. Wild and domestic animal carcasses were hauled to the area for use as attractants and trap bait, but the bear would not be fooled. Poison-bait stations were set, but the bear ignored them and ate the other, non-poisonous attractants. Hunters tracked the bear to shoot him, but they couldn't get close enough. By fall, after three to four months of steady, intensive efforts by wildlife-management agencies, the grizzly was still at large. Then, during the spring of the following year, he was killed by a hunter in a legal hunt in British Columbia. At that time, his weight was determined to be about 900 pounds.

The actions of that North Fork bear were a bit extreme, but they show how hard a bear can be to deter. Let's imagine that a bear is on your property, in your yard, at the door of your residence, or attacking your pets and livestock. You are now in a position for a surprise encounter, or to be a threat if you enter into the bear's comfort zone. Maybe your visitor is a sow with cubs. With any luck, you just observe the bear at a distance, but it is already close enough to be in conflict with you and your property. What do you do when faced with such a situation?

Despite your efforts, you have entered a more immediate and dangerous aspect of outwitting bears. A conflict has occurred, and you must resolve it.

Have a Plan

A vital element of resolving conflicts is having a plan for how to react to any bear in your area. Plan how you will resolve any problems a bear may cause. You don't need a written plan, but at least *think* about the various scenarios that might occur. Here are just a few things you might ask yourself.

How will I know a bear is on my property?
How will I react?
How will I scare away a bear? What will I use to repel a
   bear?

Are my deterrent systems (fences, lights, and so forth) in
  place?
Are noisemakers available?
Is "bear spray" available?
How will I get into and out of my house, if necessary, when
  a bear is in the area?
Where are the secure locations on my property—other
  buildings or vehicles?
How will I protect children and others? Do family mem-
  bers know how to react to a bear's presence?
How will I control and protect my dogs and other pets?
How will I protect my livestock?
Are the telephone numbers of the wildlife-management
  agency and other emergency services readily available?

Detecting Bears

There are a variety of methods to detect bears approaching
or entering your property. Simple awareness—the observation of a bear or bear sign—will often let you detect a bear's
presence. Sometimes, though, you need other, more so-
phisticated means to know when a bear is approaching.

Motion and Sound Sensors

Various motion- or sound-sensor systems can warn you of
the presence of an animal. These systems detect any movement and activate an alarm or light that warns the resident

of the presence of something and possibly frightens the intruder away.

Trip Wire

This system employs a wire strung around an area. An intruder contacts the wire, breaking an electrical (9-volt DC) circuit, triggering an alarm or lights.

Conventional Security Systems

These commercial systems are commonly utilized in residential and business situations to provide personal and property security. They are portable, easy to use, and readily available from your local security-system companies.

All sound, motion, and trip-wire systems are capable of activating a variety of deterrents, such as lights and sounds, but all have a common drawback. They do not discriminate (though some are adjustable for the size of an object), and therefore may detect *anything:* a bear, deer, person, mouse, cow, dog, cat, horse, opossum, owl, or vehicle. These systems detect bears, but they also produce a lot of false alarms.

Dogs

Dogs are aware of bears long before people even see them, and can be an excellent detection system. Any dog may detect a bear, bark, whine, and provide a warning of a bear's presence. It is up to you to detect the dog's warning, pay attention, and respond to the message.

Deterring and Chasing Away Bears

Many methods used to deter bears from approaching and entering your residential and agricultural areas have much in common with those used to chase them away. Whatever methods you use to deter or expel bears, seek advice from your local wildlife-management agency as you plan your actions. Keep in mind: Many methods that deter and chase black bears are not successful with brown bears.

Humans

People prevent most bears from approaching merely with normal activities—their noise and movements, and often mere presence. Scarecrows have deterred bears, but must be moved often to remain effective.

Bears may be chased away by a person shouting (not screaming, which may incite a bear to attack) and throwing rocks and other objects. Bears are normally shy of horses, and chasing them on horseback is often successful. They are sometimes chased by vehicles (with the horn blaring).

Dogs

Several types of dogs are used in Canada and the United States to deter bears. But the success of using dogs depends on the training of the canines. *Are* they trained, and if so, for what purpose? Any dog expected to detect and deter bears must be alert and responsive. Chase dogs must, in addition, be well trained and have experience with bears. There are trained and aggressive guard dogs used with livestock that will chase and attack bears. But take note: Some dogs have silently and prudently hidden, or slept, during a bear's visit.

Nearly all dogs, trained or untrained, tethered or contained in a yard or house, will bark or growl at the sight and scent of a bear. Confined or tethered dogs may chase away a bear by simply barking. Dogs trained to chase, and under control, will expel most black bears from the area. However, brown bears are often not as inclined to run. Loose and untrained pet dogs may cause serious problems by chasing and then provoking the bear into a reciprocal chase, and small, yappy dogs appear to aggravate bears, causing aggression.

The desire and ability of dogs to chase cars, trucks, squirrels, rabbits, other dogs, and bicycles does *not* qualify them to chase bears. Owners should know the intelligence, aptitudes, and competence of their dogs, as well as their own ability to control them.

Types of "Bear Dogs"

Guard dogs:　These specialized dogs are trained to detect and aggressively chase away bears, protecting livestock and residential areas.

Hound dogs: Normally well trained and used for hunting bears—tracking and treeing—these dogs are excellent in detecting a bear's presence and wailing loudly to serve notice to the resident as well as to the bear. They will chase black bears, tree them, and hold them at bay.

Chase dogs: Consisting of a variety of breeds, these well-trained dogs chase and retreat on command. Chasing with dogs is most successful with black bears, and probably not advisable with brown bears unless the dogs are well, and very specifically, trained. Many brown bears will hold their ground, and your chase becomes a major conflict. Remember, when the chase is reversed and the bear is now pursuing your dog, the dog may be killed, or you may end up with both dog and bear in your lap. Steve Herrero, in *Bear Attacks,* tells of just that type of situation: ". . . his dog ran over and started barking at them [bears]. As the mother bear rushed at the dog it returned to its master, bringing the enraged bear with it."

Karelian bear dogs: These are a fearless breed developed in Russia and Finland to confront and pursue bears. They are excellent trackers, and their agility and quickness allow them to avoid the direct attack of a bear. They have only recently become popular in the United States and Canada, and for the most part are used only on leashes as deterrents and in aversive conditioning.

Pet dogs: Some pets may be trained to chase and return on command, but most serve best in the roles of detection, warning, and deterrent. Their success as chase dogs is highly questionable, because most owners do not normally have time for the necessary extensive training.

Regardless of your dogs' "bear training," if they are contained or controlled they will provide you with some detection and deterrence, and their presence and barking just might chase off a bear.

Donkeys and Llamas

Llamas and donkeys have been used to protect sheep from coyotes and dogs. They are pastured with the sheep, and will harass and chase intruders. However, their defense against a black bear is highly questionable, and against a brown bear extremely doubtful. Llama and donkey owners, along with wildlife managers across the continent, say they have no evidence of donkeys and llamas protecting livestock from bears. One individual said, "Any bear, especially a brown bear, would probably consider a llama a long-neck sheep."

Fences

Fences are highly successful deterrents, *if* bears are not completely conditioned to a food source before the fence is erected. Fencing your garbage-storage area after bears have been regularly eating garbage at that site will probably not work—the bears will attack and defeat the fence to reach that familiar and reliable food source. This is an excellent example of why bears should be outwitted from the beginning, and not allowed to become conditioned to unnatural (human) foods.

Chain-Link Fences

Chain-link and high-tensile-strength wire fences are successful in deterring bears, but are also quite costly. But one of these sturdy fences installed around a residential yard may be cost-effective by providing general security, containing children and pets, protecting pools, and deterring domestic and wild animals, as well as bears.

Some people have used eight-foot-high woven-wire or chain-link fences with two feet buried in the ground, and a barbed-wire or smooth electrical-wire outrigger extension on top. Effective, but quite expensive.

Electric Fences

Electric fences are commonly used to deter bears. They are inexpensive (some cost only $200 to $300, including posts, insulators, and wire) and highly efficient if properly installed and maintained. After good sanitation and proper handling of all foods and garbage, the single most practical and effective deterrent of bears is an electric fence.

The fence energizers are powered by 6- or 12-volt batteries, flashlight batteries, 110-volt AC, or by a solar-power panel. The energizer units deliver a powerful jolt—high voltage, low amperage—that is a painful, but safe shock to bears and people. Some models, with a multi-wire fence, are effective for sixty miles.

The solar-powered units are compact, lightweight, and ideal for remote areas. A small battery is maintained by the solar panel, and provides excellent protection. These units provide power to a multi-wire fence for up to a ten-acre enclosure, or approximately one mile of line.

One design of electric fence that has been very successful is constructed of welded wire-mesh panels, fifty-two inches high and eight or ten feet wide, with a three-wire electric fence attached to the outside of the panels. The welded-wire panels add expense and therefore may not be feasible to enclose large tracts of land.

An extremely successful, but very expensive electric fence is constructed of nine high-tensile wires six inches apart, with the hot (charged) wires alternated with the ground wires. The fence is fifty-two inches tall.

There is debate over whether you should place a bait within the wires to cause a bear to place its nose on the fence. Some individuals feel it is necessary to shock a bear, while others believe the bait is merely another attractant.

Electric fences are used to protect feed-storage areas, chicken coops, rabbit hutches, small and large pastures, corrals, beehives, orchards (even individual trees), garbage containers and areas, and bird feeders. They should be used wherever possible to protect anything that might attract a bear. The full value of an electric fence includes the conditioning that a bear receives when an attractant is associated with pain (the electrical shock). Bears are often chased away from the area by the shock.

Electric fences may be used in conjunction with other deterrents in conditioning a bear to remain away from an attractant. Bears clawing at bear-resistant buildings and containers can be shocked and repelled by a temporary electric fence. The bear doesn't get a reward, and the electric shock is further reinforcement to stay away.

Wildlife-management agencies provide specifications and guidance for the installation and use of electric fences, and some offices have loaners for your emergency use. Electric fences should be used and located so that people, especially children, will not inadvertently come in contact with them.

Noise

Sound is a commonly used means of deterring and chasing bears. Success depends on an individual bear's previous experience with such deterrents. Bears learn quickly and become familiar with sounds, especially if they are repetitious. Use a variety of sounds and randomly alternate their source.

Human Voices

Talk, yell, or communicate by any vocal means to deter and chase a bear away. However, if you are in a close confrontation with a bear, you may need to be more quiet and less aggressive. (Refer to "Bear Aggression" in this chapter.)

Banging Objects Together

Clanging any two metal objects (pots, pans, metal bars, tools, cans) may prevent a bear from approaching, and even cause it to flee. Even two wood objects clacking together may be effective.

Cracker Shells

These are essentially large firecrackers shot from a 12-gauge shotgun and propelled toward a bear. It explodes with a loud explosion, and should chase away the bear. Be certain the cracker lands and explodes *between* you and the bear. If it lands beyond the bear, the obvious occurs—the bear is chased back to you, and is now considerably more irritated. Cracker shells are an excellent chase tool, but also be aware that they can start a fire by landing in flammable materials.

Flare Cartridges

These projectiles are shot from a flare pistol and explode, near the bear, with a bright flash. They are reliable, inexpensive, and portable, and they have been successful in chasing off bears.

Thunderflashes

Thunderflashes are large, hand-thrown "firecrackers" that produce a very loud "bang." Their successful use requires that you be relatively close to a bear, or have an extremely strong throwing arm. Remember, do *not* throw thunderflashes beyond a bear.

Firecrackers

Fourth of July firecrackers set off in the vicinity of a bear should at least startle it, and may deter and chase it away.

Air Horns

These are hand-held compressed-air canisters with attached horns. They are basically designed as boat horns, and they emit a loud, blaring, and very irritating sound. Air horns have been effective in face-to-face encounters, as well as in other deterrent situations.

Gunshots

Firearms discharged into the air, and away from any person, structure, or object, produce a sudden and loud noise that serves as a deterrent. There are a few hazards associated with this method of chasing off bears. The use of firearms by persons inexperienced with them is a potential hazard to other people, property, the bear, and themselves. Discharging a firearm may be illegal where you live.

Your neighbors and law-enforcement authorities may be unhappy if structures and people are in range of a bullet. And you may very well attract bears that have learned that gunshots mean a "gut pile," the remnants of an animal killed by a hunter.

Electronic Sirens

These deterrents are actually emergency-vehicle sirens that emit a variety of yelps, wails, screams, and other variations of siren sounds. They may be activated manually, or automatically by sensors.

Musical Instruments

Play any brass or reed instrument available—loudly. However, music is probably best used in the form of recordings and good speakers, unless you simply enjoy sitting outside playing a musical instrument in a bear's face.

Propane Cannons

These are timed devices that build up a propane charge and are automatically ignited. They emit loud, repeated blasts.

Taped Sounds

Any sound may be recorded and played back at appropriate times and at high volume. You can even hook up a tape player to motion and sound sensors, or to a timer. Speakers can easily be moved from place to place. This system is simple and effective, but possibly not of long-term value with the same bear. Sounds used to deter or chase bears must be acceptable to your neighbors, or you will have another type of problem.

Lights

Many bears avoid lights at night, secretly moving under the cover of darkness. Therefore, any type of light can be an effective deterrent. Bears will generally avoid well-lighted areas around your residence, barn, outbuildings, parked vehicles, yards, corrals, and any other places where you do not want them.

Motion-sensor security lights are very inexpensive and simple to install. They provide a sudden, very bright light that covers a 50- to 75-foot area. The light is quite startling and effective, if pointed directly at the bear when activated.

Bright flashlights or strobe lights will act as a deterrent to a bear entering an area.

Rubber Bullets, Rubber Buckshot, and Plastic Slugs

These projectiles are shot from a 12-gauge shotgun, and strike a bear in the heavily muscled areas, causing pain. They are effective in deterring bears as well as providing aversive conditioning.

Chemicals

Pepper Spray

This is a Capsaicin, red-pepper-based spray delivered from an aerosol canister, designed for face-to-face conflicts with bears, and normally not carried unless you are traveling in bear country. However, I strongly recommend you have one or two of the largest size. They should be readily available—essentially in your hands—when you are resolving a bear "situation" anywhere on your property. Anyone living in bear country should have bear spray available.

The spray irritates a bear's eyes and nasal passages. The canister's effective range is a maximum of thirty feet (some brands considerably less), so you need to be relatively close. The chemical has been quite successful in turning away a charging bear. But it is not perfect, and you should take all possible measures to prevent ever having to use bear spray.

Do not use "pepper spray" as a deterrent applied on structures, objects, or the ground, as there is substantial evidence that in this type of application the spray serves as an attractant.

Ammonia

This cleanser has caustic fumes, and is spread in garbage-storage areas and cans as a deterrent and sanitizer. It is only moderately effective because the irritating fumes dissipate rapidly, but it masks other odors considerably longer.

Lime

Lime masks odors that attract bears and is placed in garbage cans and outhouses. It has more long-term value than ammonia.

Repellents

A variety of commercial products are sold as repellents to be sprayed on vegetation, around buildings, and on any other area with attractants. I have not found these sprays to be more than moderately successful with numerous types of wild and domestic animals. The repellent is quickly removed by rain, frost, irrigation systems, and lawn sprinklers.

Bear-proof Structures

Buildings are bear deterrents if solidly constructed, though they are the last line of defense. Walls should preferably be concrete, but log and framed structures made of heavy materials are also bear-resistant, and more practical.

Normally, the portions of a structure most vulnerable to bear entry are doors and windows. All doors should have heavily constructed outer doors that seat tightly within the frames—so tightly that a bear cannot hook a claw in a crack. Windows should have shutters constructed and installed in the same manner. All shutters and doors must be strongly hinged and latched. These types of doors and windows are not practical for continually occupied residences, and therefore other deterrent measures become even more important.

Bear-proof Containers

Fifty-five-gallon drums, with locking snap rings to secure the lids, will protect small quantities of livestock foods and other attractants. The tight-fitting lids reduce odors, but this type of container should also be stored in a building if at all possible.

Numerous types of recently developed bear-resistant storage containers and boxes are available commercially. They are constructed of 12-gauge steel, with tight-fitting lids or doors, and are available in several designs and sizes. They have been highly successful in making animal feed, people food, and garbage unavailable to bears. Contact your local wildlife agency for guidance as to types and the nearest sources.

Aversive Conditioning

Aversive conditioning is an action that causes a bear to associate a place, situation, dogs, or humans with a painful or frightening experience. This deterrent is normally performed by wildlife-management agencies, though you may actually provide an unpleasant condition for a bear with your basic deterrent measures, as previously described. These measures include:

Fireworks thrown at the bear, or simply exploded in the area.
Cracker shells fired from a shotgun.
Chase dogs that are well trained to chase away a bear, avoiding an attack.
Electric fences.
Pepper spray, when effectively utilized.
Rubber bullets.
Rubber buckshot.
Plastic slugs.

Chasing Bears

Chasing away a bear does not involve running behind the animal, yelling at it, and forcing it to flee the area forever. You chase away a bear by doing something (from a safe location) that causes the bear to leave the area at whatever pace it desires. As a bear departs you may wish to carefully follow, continuing your actions, but with a secure retreat available. If you chase a bear by vehicle, on horseback, or with dogs, you may be able to more aggressively and safely pursue it.

Many chasing methods are those also used to deter bears. However, they are not the aversive-conditioning measures that are physical and painful. Bears are chased with a variety of methods, including:

Air horns.
A shock from an electric fence.
Bear spray (in a face-to-face situation).
Bright or flashing lights.

Chase dogs.
Barking dogs.
Propane cannons.
Fireworks.
Road flares.
Gunfire (shots fired into the air, or taped gunshots).
Human presence.
Human voices (taped or actual).
Loud music.
Loud noise (such as banging metal pots together).
People on horseback.
People shouting (not screaming).
Throwing rocks and other objects.
People in vehicles.
A person on horseback.
Projectiles (rubber bullets and buckshot, and plastic slugs).
Cracker shells.
Sirens.
Sprinkler systems.
Taped noise of any type.
Vehicles driven at a bear (with the horns blowing).
Vehicle horns.

Neighbors

Now a few words of caution. Many of the above actions and measures may not be appreciated by your neighbors. They would need to be extremely tolerant to withstand continual explosions, blaring horns, loud music, sirens, and gun-shots. Work closely with your neighbors as you apply your outwitting measures. They also benefit from your actions, and probably should be taking the same measures at their homes.

Property Damage

When you return home to find a shed broken into by a bear, or wake up to find your garbage strewn across the yard, you need to take action right away. Promptly clean up all messes, hosing down areas if necessary. Stay alert: the bear is probably nearby. Begin repairs if necessary. If rebuilding or repairing a structure is necessary, consider an improved, bear-resistant construction.

During your cleanup, determine where things went wrong. Unsecured human, dog, or livestock foods? Garbage left out? Inadequate "bear-resistant" structures? Begin your outwitting process again, and improve your measures to prevent attracting bears.

Report the incident to your local wildlife-management agency, seeking assistance in resolving the situation and improving your security measures. Inform your neighbors of a bear's presence.

Storage Areas

If a bear breaks into a storage building, shed, or fenced area, it will most likely remove or scatter most if not all of the attractants. When the bear is gone, clean up the area and then move all remaining garbage, foods, chemicals, and debris to another secure area. Use ammonia or a deodorizer to scrub down your original storage area (lime may also aid in deterring further bear investigation), and leave it open and available to the bear. When the bear returns, it will find a deterrent odor, but no reward, and it should soon move on. Wait at least a week before resuming use of that storage area. You may want to use an electric fence around your temporary storage building, moving it to the permanent facility when you resume use of that area.

Livestock

If a bear comes into your livestock area and injures or kills animals, chase it away if possible. Notify the local wildlife-management agency and your neighbors. Move the livestock to more secure holding areas and increase your deterrent measures, such as electric fences, dogs, and lighting around buildings. Keep the animals inside a secure barn, stable, or shed at night, and monitor them closely day and night until the immediate threat is gone. Ranchers should monitor their more remote herds, and move them to other pastures or secure holding areas if there is a persistent problem.

The laws regulating the killing of a bear caught in the act of destroying livestock vary from state to state. Discuss such situations with your wildlife-management agencies in advance, and know the proper and legal actions.

A Bear in the Yard

When you observe a black bear on your property or in your yard, do not panic, but make your presence known. Stand upright and be "big." Most bears will normally leave when in the presence of people. If it does not depart on its own, shout at the bear and make loud noises by banging pots or other metal objects. Attempt to chase it off as you would a stray dog entering your yard. Do not run directly up to a bear, and be certain it has an escape route. If this does not work, retreat into a secure building and leave the bear alone. If the bear climbs a tree, leave it alone, and remove any dogs and people from the area so it will have the opportunity to come down out of the tree and depart.

If the intruder is a brown bear, remain in a secure location and use cautious attempts—shouting, banging pans—to frighten it away. Brown bears are normally not deterred as easily as black bears.

If the bear makes a mess, scatters garbage, or otherwise causes damage, clean up after it departs, and be certain that whatever attracted and rewarded the bear is removed. Notify your local wildlife management agency.

Surprise Encounters

What if your first knowledge of or contact with a bear is a face-to-face encounter? You meet in your yard or just outside the back door of your house, most likely in the dark. If the bear is investigating, its normal reaction will be to flee the area, or at least run away from you. As it does, be certain that you are in a safe location and that the bear has an escape route. Chase it off as described in the previous segment, with noise and stationary aggression.

But what if the bear does not flee? What if it shows aggression? What if it is a brown bear? Your conflict has been elevated to a higher level of intensity and danger. Begin talking to the bear (say anything, just talk) in a soft voice—calm, assuring, but assertive—so as not to threaten the bear. Slowly back away, avoiding direct eye contact, which may be perceived by the bear as a threat. Always leave the bear an escape route. You should at this moment be seeking a secure and safe location.

Bear Aggression

If a bear does not flee upon being surprised or when confronted in a residential area, and feels threatened and becomes aggressive, you have some quick decisions to make and important actions to take. How you react will depend on which species of bear you have encountered. Bear attacks are rare, but they do occur, and each situation is unique. Nearly every attack happens because the bear feels threatened and is interested in protecting food, cubs, or its "personal" space. Usually, aggression is terminated when the threats are removed, and the bear leaves. Each of the following situations applies to both brown and black bears.

A Bear Observed at a Distance and *Not* Aware of You

You should:

Not make abrupt moves or noises that would startle it and
 alert it to your presence.
Slowly move to a secure building or vehicle.
Attempt to observe the bear's actions and note where it
 travels.

A Distant Bear That Is Aware of You

If the bear flees, you should:

Remain calm.
Ready your canister of bear spray.
Not approach or pursue the bear.
Not run.
Shout and make noises as it flees.
Move to a secure area.
Watch where the bear proceeds as it flees.

If the bear stays put, it might stand on its hind legs to
better identify you. Standing improves its scent and view of
you. Its head may turn from side to side while bipedal; this
is not an aggressive posture. If a bear acts this way, you
should:

Remain calm.
Ready your canister of bear spray.
Not approach the bear.

Not run.

Call other people to join you if they are nearby; several individuals appear more formidable and better deter a bear.

Allow the bear to determine what you are by waving your arms and talking to it in a normal, firm, monotone voice.

Not make noises or abrupt movements that could startle or threaten the bear and provoke an attack.

Walk to a secure building or vehicle.

If the bear runs toward you, it may only be approaching for better identification. In this case, you should:

Remain calm.

Prepare your canister of bear spray.

Not run, but back away, diagonally if possible; a diagonal retreat provides a stronger impression of retreat, lessening the threat.

Immediately move into a secure building or vehicle, if one is close. Remember that a bear running 30 mph covers 44 feet per second.

Do not make abrupt movements or loud noises that might threaten the bear and provoke an attack.

Allow the bear to determine what you are by slowly waving your arms and talking to it in a normal, firm, monotone voice.

Drop an item of diversion, but not food, as you back away.

Continue to seek safety in a building or vehicle.

The Close Encounter

If a bear comes close and stands on its hind legs, it may identify you, not display aggression, and leave. Or it might look toward you, its head turning from side to side as it tries to identify you. If a bear does this, you should:

Remain calm. Do not panic; quick movements may also cause the bear to panic.
Have your canister of bear spray ready.
Not run.
Not make abrupt movements or loud noises that might threaten the bear and provoke an attack.
Talk to the bear in a normal, firm, monotone voice.
Back away, diagonally if possible. Stop moving away if doing so appears to agitate the bear—if it clacks its teeth or jaws and/or makes moaning, woofing, or barking sounds.
Retreat to safety if you are standing *next to* the door of a secure building or vehicle.

If you are facing a black bear that does not have cubs, attempt to chase it off with mild aggression—yell, shout (do not scream), blow a whistle, throw something, or bang metal objects together. Do not be timid. Do not respond this way if it is a brown bear or any sow with cubs. Keep moving to a secure area if you are able to back out of sight.

If the bear approaches on all four legs, this is an aggressive approach. The bear may swing its head from side to side in a display of nervousness and agitation. If it presents a side view of its body as if ignoring you, the bear is expressing dominance, but is reluctant to charge—though it may still do so—and is seeking a way out of the situation. A bear that looks directly at you with its ears back is expressing a warning that it feels crowded and threatened. It may further emphasize its distress with barking, woofing, or moaning sounds. If the bear clacks its jaws and teeth together, gives a series of woofs, or both, it is highly agitated and quite likely to charge.

In this situation, you should:

Not run. Stay calm—it is *not* easy, but very necessary.

Have had your canister of bear spray ready long ago.

Avoid direct eye contact with the bear.

Talk to the bear in a normal, firm, monotone voice.

Not imitate a bear's sounds, actions, or motions.

Not turn your back on the bear.

Back away. Give the bear space and an escape route. Attempt to reduce the bear's feeling of being crowded, even though it approached you. Retreat to safety.

Stop moving away if doing so agitates the bear. Begin backing away again when the agitation ceases.

If the animal is a black bear *without cubs,* attempt to chase it off with mild aggression—yell, shout (do not scream), blow a whistle, throw rocks or sticks, or bang metal objects together. Do not be timid. Do not respond this way if it is a brown bear or any sow with cubs. If you are able to back out of sight, keep moving into a secure area.

If the bear charges you, it might mean to attack, or it might be bluffing. It may veer off, run by you, or stop: *this is an attempt to scare you away.* The bear might leave after several bluff charges. But while there may be no contact with you at this moment, there is a fine line between a bluff charge and an actual attack.

If you have bear spray—and it should have been ready for use long ago—you should:

Remain calm. Do not run.
Use the bear spray.
If others with you have spray, they too should spray the bear—the more the better.
Slowly retreat to a secure location.

If you *do not* have bear spray, if it does not affect the bear, or if the canister malfunctions, you should:

Remain calm. Do not run (this is one of the greatest challenges of your life).
Attempt to reduce the bear's feeling of being threatened (even though you may have already hit it in the face with pepper spray) by not making aggressive movements or sounds.
Avoid direct eye contact with the bear.
Not yell, shout, or scream, but continue talking in a normal, firm, monotone voice.

Not kick, strike, or lash out at the bear.

Throw an object on the ground as a diversion, including an empty pepper spray can, and back away from it.

Back away and retreat to safety if the bear makes a bluff charge.

If the aggressor is a black bear without cubs, attempt to chase it off with mild aggression—look big and dominant, wave your arms, yell, shout (do not scream), blow a whistle, throw something, or bang metal objects together. Do not be timid. If the bear does not depart within a minute, back away and retreat to safety. Do not respond this way if it is a brown bear or any sow with cubs.

In all situations, remain calm—do not panic. At best, panic results in a charge. When you are in a safe location, building, or vehicle, be sure to tell others in your area about the aggressive bear. Immediately contact your local wildlife-management agency.

The Bear Attack

Bears attack other animals and humans for two basic purposes: for food and as a defensive reaction. Other than when preying on wild animals, bears rarely attack. A bear would rather bluff to scare away an intruder, or flee. But if it attacks, the situation is dire.

When you believe a bear is going to make contact with you, spray it in the face. Don't give it just a single burst of fog—empty the canister. Hit the bear in the face as it approaches, based on the range of your canister. Ideally, the bear will back off and you can retreat to security.

But, if the bear makes physical contact with you, continue spraying it in the face if at all possible. If you do not have bear spray, or if it did not repel the bear, your actions should be based on the species of bear.

If the aggressor is a black bear, *fight back*. Be aggressive and defend yourself with everything available. Appear dominant and try to frighten the bear. Fight with your feet, fists, sticks, noise, rocks, shovels, laundry baskets—whatever weapons are available. Strike, kick, gouge, bite—you are fighting for your life. If other people are in the house or close by, call for their help; their presence alone may cause the bear to terminate the attack.

If the attacking bear is a brown bear, including a grizzly bear, *play dead*. Fall to the ground as the bear actually touches you, but not until then. Either lie flat on your stomach, or, as some bear biologists and managers recommend, drop to the ground with your legs up underneath your chest, and bend forward so your forehead touches your kneecaps, assuming the cannonball or fetal position.

Once on the ground, try to remember the following measures:

Keep your arms bent forward alongside and around your head to protect your face and head.
Clasp your hands, interlocking the fingers over the back of your neck.

Do not struggle, fight, or attempt to restrain the bear—*remain motionless.*

Do not cry out or make any noise—*remain silent.*

If the bear swats or paws you, turning you over, roll back onto your stomach, keeping your hands and arms clasped around your head at all times.

Remain motionless and silent for at least twenty minutes (though that may not be enough) to allow the bear time to leave.

If an attack is renewed, play dead again.

If an attack persists—if you believe the bear is not going to leave you or it is preying upon you—you should:

Attempt to get away.

Shout for help.

Fight for your life in the same way as if the aggressor were a black bear.

Be aggressive and defend yourself with everything available.

Fighting has often turned away a black bear, and occasionally deterred a brown bear. This may seem strange and desperate, but if a bear will not cease attacking you, fighting back may be your only chance.

Let us hope you never face this scenario. Living in bear country includes responsibilities and risks, and occasionally serious consequences. If you concentrate on the responsibilities, the conflicts will be minimized, if not eliminated. Begin with good methods to deter a bear from entering your property.

Six

Living with Polar Bears

". . . there are Bears which are called Amphibia, because they live both on the Land and in the Sea, hunting and catching fish like an Otter or Beaver, and these are white coloured."
  —Edward Topsell, *The History of Four-footed Beasts* (1607)

The "wandering bear," of monstrous size, was called a polar bear—Nanook by the early Native Americans—long before the North Pole was discovered. Considered by many the most dangerous species of bear—a formidable adversary specialized for killing—polar bears are one of North America's most magnificent animals. According to Charles Feazel, in *White Bear,* "No human, nothing in nature, challenges their supremacy; in the darkness of winter, the ice belongs to Nanook."

The arctic is sparsely populated with people, but most of those who live there are intensely involved in a life of coexistence with polar bears, living with and outwitting them (or maybe I should say outwitting them in order to live with them). The measures to outwit Nanook are for the most part very different from the challenge of outwitting black and brown bears.

Most of the readers of this book will never travel above the Arctic Circle, north into the habitat of these white bears, and therefore will not need to outwit them. So, I've provided polar bears their own chapter, one that presents the magnificence and uniqueness of these tireless travelers of the North. The purpose is not to tell you how to live with polar bears, but to explain how the people and bears of the Far North coexist.

Evolution of Polar Bears

Polar bears are specialized descendants of the brown bear, and the youngest of the living species of bears. They began evolving between 100,000 and 50,000 years ago somewhere along the Siberian coast, where they split off from the Asian brown bear population. They may have appeared about 70,000 years ago as a distinct species adapted to the sea.

Their evolutionary changes are extreme. They have evolved from land occupants to residents of the sea, from brown to white in color, and from omnivores, with a mostly herbaceous diet, to carnivores that feed primarily on seals. They are true predators.

Distribution and Populations

Polar bears are generally grouped in six closed populations on the southern edge of the Arctic ice cap: Canadian archipelago; Greenland; northern Alaska; Siberia; Spitsbergen–Franz Josef Land; and Wrangel Island to western Alaska. The world population consists of between 35,000 and 40,000 bears. The United States has approximately 2,000, located entirely in Alaska. In Canada, there are more than 15,000, in Manitoba, Newfoundland, Ontario, Quebec, the Northwest Territories, and the Yukon Territory.

The polar bear's distribution is circumpolar. Even though they are known for their extensive wanderings, polar bears have been thought to remain in specific geographical areas during most of their lifetime. However, recent evidence may indicate greater movement and more exchange between the groups. Their home ranges, some 20,000 square miles, are larger than those of any land bear.

Natural History

Arctic explorer Peter Freuchen, in Ben East's *Bears,* said of polar bears that "No more beautiful animal walks on four feet."

A polar bear's body is elongated, with a lean, smallish, flat head, a long, relatively thin but powerful neck, low, well-muscled shoulders, and heavy hindquarters. It has a straight profile and a Roman nose with a bulge at the bridge of the snout. Its feet are very large, with membranes up to one half the length of the toes, and immense claws that are long, thick, and black. The paws are built for swimming, shoveling snow, and traveling on and through snow and ice. Four inches of blubber cover the rump and legs, except inside the back legs.

Polar bears are the largest of the bears, though occasionally they are not considered as large as brown bears, due to their shape—thinner head and more streamlined shoulders—and smaller skull measurements. Charles Feazel describes them this way: ". . . the largest predators that stalk the earth. . . . If he wished Nanook could slap a giraffe in the face."

The average weight of adult male polar bears is 1,150 pounds, with a range from 900 to 1,600. The heaviest recorded weight is 2,210 pounds. Their average life span is twenty-five years, and the oldest age ever determined in the wild was thirty-four years and eight months.

Polar bears are the most fur-clad species of bears, completely covered except for nose and paw pads; the fur is thick with tufted guard hairs. Their hollow oily hair, two to six inches long, provides heat preservation while on land and buoyancy at sea, and is not white or yellow as it appears, but transparent. The hair has no insulating value when in the sea.

Agility, Quickness, and Strength

Polar bears possess amazing agility. They are quite capable of climbing, scrambling up onto and over huge blocks of ice and ice ridges, and scaling six-foot-high ice barriers. They have been observed to jump down ten feet, scale a thirty-five-foot ice wall, and climb onto village buildings and through high windows in houses. They are capable of leaping out of the water up to eight feet in the air from a swimming start, and onto an ice floe, usually in an attempt to kill a basking seal.

Like other bears, they possess enormous strength. An adult polar bear can move ice blocks weighing hundreds of pounds, smash and dig through three-foot-thick ice to reach a seal pup, and tear off doors and walls of buildings while seeking human foods.

Behavior

Disposition and Personality

Polar bears have had, for the most part, less contact with humans than other bears have had. Therefore they have less fear of people, and are more dangerous. Silent and cunning, with a casual demeanor, they are fierce fighters. "Untrustworthy" best describes them in captivity. Phyllis Osteen, in *Bears Around The World,* describes polar bears as having "the touchiest temper of all bears."

They are solitary, but often tolerate close associations when they feed on large food supplies, such as a whale carcass. They occasionally play together.

Intelligence

Polar bears have been considered less intelligent than grizzly bears, but a variety of evidence indicates they are highly intelligent and cunning. They have been known to prepare a seal's hole so it is large enough for a paw, and then wait in ambush for the seal. Strong evidence has existed for over 200 years that polar bears use ice blocks or rocks as "tools" to kill seals, and they have been known to use small rocks to spring traps.

They use a number of feeding strategies and tools, according to Feazel. They "push ice or snow blocks ahead of them as they slither close to the breathing holes . . . build walls of snow to hide behind and they use blocks of ice to smash through the icy crust that covers a [seal's] breathing hole." They have been known to throw a rock, from above, onto the head of a walrus, stunning it until they inflict the final death blow with a massive paw.

Mark Rosenthal, a curator at Chicago's Lincoln Park Zoo, relates an example of a polar bear's intelligence in Charles Feazel's *White Bear:*

> [He] would eat his food [a meat mixture] but would always leave a few scraps on the floor. Then he'd lie down with his paws forward like a dog, rest his chin on the ground, and pretend to be asleep. The food scraps were just inches in front of his nose. What he was doing was waiting for pigeons. When one would land to peck at the scraps, . . . [he] would make a grab. Now and then he'd actually get one.

Curiosity

The curiosity of polar bears may be more focused than that of other bears; so few objects appear on the ice that they investigate every one, especially since most if not all are food. The true value of their curiosity is the discovery of the most nutritious sources of food.

Senses

Vision

Polar bears have specialized eyes that provide very adaptable and excellent vision exceeding that of other bear species. Their eyes are large, almost as large as human eyes, and have an extra eyelid—nictitating membrane— that protects them, keeping them clean and moist, filtering snow glare, and providing good underwater vision. Their depth perception, night vision, and distance vision are excellent.

Smell

Like that of all other bear species, a polar bear's sense of smell is outstanding—its key to its surroundings. Terry Domico, in *Bears of The World,* best describes a polar bear's olfactory senses: ". . . male polar bears march in a straight line, over the tops of pressure ridges of uplifted ice . . . up to 40 miles to reach a prey animal they had detected."

Hearing

Polar bears' ears are small, located low on their heads for a low profile and protection, and furred inside to guard against the cold. The ear canals close while underwater.

Their hearing is extremely sensitive, able to detect seal pups below several feet of solid ice.

Hibernation

Males and non-pregnant females do not hibernate. Pregnant females hibernate from late October to late March or early April. They dig dens in ice and snow, or use crevices of ice ridges. Most are within five miles of the coast.

Reproduction

These huge white bears of the Arctic have one of the earliest estrus periods of all bears, breeding during a three-week period in April and May. Feazel, in *White Bear*, says, "The ultimate social interaction is finding a mate. Mating itself is a brief act."

The gestation period is 240 to 270 days. One or two cubs (10 percent of litters have three cubs) are born in late November to early January.

Motherhood

Like all other bears, a polar bear sow is an extremely devoted mother, nursing her cubs fifteen minutes at a time, six to seven times a day. The polar bear's milk has an odor of fish. It contains 30 percent milk fat (whole milk from the supermarket has 4 percent milk fat), and has the consistency of condensed milk.

Traveling

Polar bears are nomadic, continually moving in search of food and traveling considerably farther than the other bears. Often remaining in the same general location, they adjust to the drifting ice pack as the ice moves under them.

Walking

The walk of a polar bear is an easy, dignified motion that covers a lot of ground. They are quite capable of picking up the pace. A tracked male bear covered 800 miles in a month, and a female traveled 205 miles in two days.

Running

Running at 25 mph (35 mph for short distances), polar bears are capable of bringing down caribou if the race is short. Running for great distances is not terribly common, though, as they easily overheat.

Swimming

The best swimmer of all bears, polar bears move through the water with exceptional power, and have excellent buoyancy, thanks to their thick, oily fur and blubber. Their shape allows them to move through the water with relative ease, normally paddling at a speed of six mph, using only their front legs, with the hind legs trailing as a rudder. (They may at times use all four legs and paws.) They leave a wake as they move through the water, and their muzzles are submerged in rough water, but are regularly raised to breathe. Polar bears can swim sixty miles without rest, and have displayed enormous endurance, swimming approximately three hundred miles between ice floes.

Habitat and Habits

Polar bear country is the Arctic—coastal regions, islands, ice, and the Arctic seas. The bears live on the dark, cold ice pack during the winters. They spend their summers offshore on the edge of the sea ice as it recedes north, and along coastlines and inland where they seek carrion and vegetation. Falls are spent moving to new ice, with many bears concentrating during October and November in several coastal areas of earliest freeze-up, where they will again move back onto the pack ice. Polar bears spend months in complete darkness, and then months in glaring sunlight, much of the time in extremely cold temperatures.

Foods and Feeding Habits

Poet and writer Joaquin Miller wrote a true story of a polar bear attempting to catch a seal. The bear spent most of a day trying various approaches and methods to capture the potential meal, but all failed. Miller relates, "The rage of the animal was boundless, it moaned hideously, tossing the snow in the air, and at last trotted off in a most indignant state of mind."

Highly efficient predators and the most carnivorous of the bears, polar bears stalk areas with open water and active movements of ice, where they are most likely to find ringed seals, their primary food. On the ice, they stand to observe and locate any dark object. Anything that is dark or moves is food.

In addition to its superb natural camouflage, this bear uses stealth and a sudden burst of speed to approach its prey. A polar bear uses the wind to its advantage, approaching directly into it, and it may use a shadow or shield such as ice blocks and ridges. It tucks its forelegs under its chest and pushes with hind legs, or pulls itself along on the ice, stopping when its prey moves or looks. A polar bear approaches closely, then with a burst of speed bounds and pounces on the prey, using its canines to grasp a seal in its hole, or its paw to strike the seal out onto the ice.

With incredible patience, a polar bear will lie beside a seal's breathing hole for hours, waiting to strike when the seal comes up for air. If in the water, it will slowly approach a seal on the ice, with only its eyes and the tip of its nose barely above the surface. Submerging, it moves closer, and then rears from the water next to the seal, killing it with a single blow of its paw to the head. This may sound quite efficient, but polar bears are successful in less than one-fourth of their attacks on seals. A single bear typically kills and eats a seal every four to five days. They have a stomach capacity of 150 pounds, and eat 100 to 150 pounds of blubber at each meal.

Whales may be killed when they are limited to small openings in the ice for breathing. The bears hunt them as they do seals in the water, lying on the ice edge and delivering a blow to the head, then grasping and hauling them onto the ice. Calves are the usual prey; Beluga whales' young average seven and a half feet long, and Narwhal's calves are similar in size. Frank Dufresne, in *No Room For Bears,* relates an interesting polar-bear hunting story: "[He] had seen a polar bear jump on the back of a surfacing whale, go down with it, and come up again still trying to bite a mouthful of blubber off the forty-ton behemoth."

Carrion—the carcasses of seals, whales, and walruses—is also an important food source all year. During the summer, when the ice is gone and seals are unavailable, polar bears eat puffins, ducks, other birds, eggs, fish, crabs, and the occasional weak caribou. Berries (often indicated by the butt and muzzle of a bear being stained bluish), algae, lichens, mosses, and grasses are also consumed when a bear cannot find anything else.

Surface melt on ice floes is a source of fresh water for polar bears. Shoreline streams provide drinking water during the summer.

Day Beds

Male bears and non-pregnant females have day beds. They scoop out depressions in the snow or sleep under ledges of ice.

Enemies

As ferocious and predatory as they are, polar bears still have enemies. Obviously, humans are a threat, with firearms, harassment, and invasion of the bear's habitat, but polar bears have a couple of natural adversaries.

The killer whale is the polar bears' greatest natural threat. Although polar bears swim six miles an hour, weigh an average of more than 1,100 pounds and are more than eight feet long, they are no match for a killer whale capable of swimming thirty miles an hour, and which is over thirty feet long and weighs in excess of eight tons. Polar bears simply avoid the orcas.

The walrus is the only polar animal that the bear actually fears. Encounters between a walrus and a polar bear are violent battles, and there are several recorded observations of a walrus killing a polar bear, though walruses are also killed. If the two animals encounter each other on land, the polar bear will have an edge. When they meet in the water, the colossal walrus, with its two- to three-foot tusks, is normally victorious.

Polar bear cubs also face the threat of male bears of their own species, as well as predation by wolves.

Living in Polar Bear Country

Ursus maritimus, the largest land carnivore, the most predatory of the bears, is obviously a challenge to live with in
bear country. In the Arctic, where the seasons are described as "winter and the Fourth of July," the polar bear
and a few people share a land covered with ice and snow
much of the year, an ocean with constantly moving ice, a
climate with extreme temperature ranges, and long periods of darkness and glaring sunlight. This is the kingdom
of the white bears, and they are well adapted to this country, while the people, for much of the time, merely survive.
Residents of the Arctic not only live with bears, but reside
in one of the harshest areas of the world.

The earliest European knowledge of polar bears dates
back approximately 1,900 years. The Inuits and Eskimos
have lived with and exploited them for many thousands of
years. Like other bears, the white bears were revered,
hunted, and used.

The early indigenous peoples' relationships with polar
bears was essentially the same as those of native peoples
elsewhere in North America. They worshipped and
treated them with incredible reverence. Nanook was a
powerful shaman, a spirit who communed with the spirit
world. In turn, the people communed with Nanook.
There were ceremonial dances to honor polar bears. The
elderly, being near death and having become a burden,
were placed out on the ice to die by the white bear—a to-
ken of respect, a sacrifice.

Killing a polar bear was a rite of passage into manhood among the Inuits of northern Canada. To be killed by a polar bear was an acceptable means of death.

Polar bears were traditionally hunted with a spear five to six feet long, with a head of jade or copper found in natural deposits. They were hunted from kayak, but on land if at all possible. When they killed a polar bear, Eskimos have been traditionally considered "master hunters." But in hunting polar bears, "predator" and "prey" are determined only by the final outcome. Richard Perry, in *Bears,* wrote, "Many Eskimos have been killed by polar bears; the great majority of them have been hunters killed while lancing or knifing bears at close-quarters."

All bears have been used by humans, but the paucity of natural resources in the Arctic has made the polar bear crucial to the livelihood of the residents. The furs have been utilized for clothing, boots, and sheathings for sledge runners. Bones were used for tools, and jewelry was made from teeth and other small parts. The meat was rarely eaten, normally as a last resort, but when dogs became the primary means of transportation, polar-bear meat was their main diet.

Explorers, Whalers and Traders

The early explorers of the northern latitudes viewed polar bears with awe. Polar bears were more bold than the bears explorers and adventurers had met elsewhere, making aggressive approaches and attacking without warning. They swam out to anchored vessels, where feeding them became a popular pastime.

They preyed on humans, killing and eating their victims, and tore open graves, tossing, rolling, and consuming the bodies. The bears destroyed equipment and supply caches, as the early land adventurers underestimated the strength of their caches and the power and determination of the bears. In Thomas Koch's *The Year of the Polar Bear,* Dr. E.K. Kane describes a mid-1800s experience:

> The final cache . . . was entirely destroyed. It had been built with extreme care, of rocks which had been assembled by very heavy labor. . . . The entire construction was . . . most effective and resisting. Not a morsel of pemmican remained except in the iron cases which, being round with conical ends, defied both claws and teeth. They had rolled and pawed them in every direction, tossing them about like footballs, although over eighty pounds in weight. An alcohol case, strongly iron-bound, was dashed into small fragments and a tin can of liquor mashed and twisted almost into a ball. The claws of the beast had perforated the metal, and torn it up as with a cold chisel.

Sealers killed the bears because they were in competition for the seals, whalers killed them for sport, and explorers because they were a threat. Polar bears were trophies.

As with other bears, the relationship between early residents of and visitors to the Arctic and the polar bears was one of strife. The personality and physical prowess of the bears prompted them to stalk, fight, and kill, but humans proved the more efficient killers. Polar-bear populations began to decline.

Military and Defense Activities in Polar Bear Country

Over the last half century, the white bears have received further affronts. Defense activities soared to a high level during the 1950s, and the construction of military facilities and systems affected the polar bears, their habitat, and activities. Military communities were established, construction workers arrived, and bears were fed, harassed, and shot. Workers returning home to areas outside the Arctic brought souvenirs—polar bear furs—for their families. More polar bears were killed to meet the growing demand. Construction, and human populations, increased as Distant Early Warning and Ballistic Missile Early Warning facilities were completed.

The polar bears were considered nuisances and predators, and were hunted not only by the Eskimos and Inuits, but by new residents and visitors as well. By the 1960s, polar bears were beginning to be hunted by air and snowmobiles, and these new hunters had more powerful rifles. More than 1,100 polar bears a year were being removed from Alaska and Canada.

Oil exploration and extraction further impacted the Arctic, and especially the polar bears. The world's polar-bear population was declining—something had to be done for them. Scientists, naturalists, wildlife managers, and much of the public had long been concerned, and now governments began to understand the plight of polar bears.

In 1965, the First International Scientific Meeting on the Polar Bear was held in Fairbanks, Alaska. Delegates attended from Canada, Norway, Denmark, the USSR, and the United States. Their discussions led to recommendations for more conservative management of polar bears.

In 1968, Canada's Northwest Territories placed quotas on polar bears taken by Native Americans, and by the early 1970s Canada and Alaska placed restrictions on all hunters. The Marine Mammals Protection Act was passed by Congress in 1972, limiting polar bear hunting in the United States to the Alaskan Eskimos.

The International Agreement on the Conservation of Polar Bears and Their Habitat was developed by five nations in 1973 to "protect the ecosystem of which polar bears are a part." Systems to conserve polar bears were finally in place.

The Present

Though they are protected from exploitation today, polar bears remain in conflict with residents of the Arctic. The problems are similar to those with black and brown bears, but the cause is the bears' persistent hunger, and not just a day-to-day search for nourishment. Polar bears and people have more close, face-to-face confrontations because of the bears' general behavior and disposition—bold and aggressive—and because they do not hibernate. Polar bears would live in town if they were allowed. A resident of Churchill, Manitoba, commented, "We are living in the polar bears' territory and like other bears they are very inquisitive creatures, the only differences are that they are not hunted and have no other competitors, so **they have an attitude.**"

As the ice melts in the spring, polar bears must move ashore, and into areas of human habitation. Without their primary food source (seals), they seek human foods. Some bears have actually adjusted to coming off the ice early and moving into towns. Most bears move on to remote areas to seek the sparse natural summer food, but some find themselves in conflicts by remaining near residences, villages, and towns.

Natural spring and summer foods are not at all sufficient for many bears, and they are extremely hungry by late summer when they move back to coastlines, where they await the development of pack ice and the availability of seals. If their migration routes place them near residences, villages, and towns, they will move into these convenient developments, seeking human foods and other nourishment. The bears appear to be seasonally conditioned to human foods, and during this period there are more intense and dangerous conflicts between people and bears. Hungry bears are obviously the most dangerous— no one is safe. Helen Thayer, in *Polar Dream*, says, "A thin-looking bear that plods directly towards you with its head down is very dangerous and hard to deter."

The polar bears investigate individual residences, villages, and towns, and communities such as Churchill, Manitoba and Point Barrow and Prudhoe Bay, Alaska, where various items attract them into conflict with people. These attractants include:

Human foods.
Meat scraps, blubber, and other hunting residue left outside residences.
Cooking water thrown outside.
Garbage and trash.
Oil and other petroleum products.
Vehicles.
Dogs (sled-dog owners who have numerous dogs seem to have very few problems with polar bears).
Dog food left outside.
Whale carcasses and gut piles.
Dumps, especially those not fenced.
Glass; they are intrigued by glass of different color shades.
Any of the same attractants found in black- and brown-bear country.

Polar bears pose a threat to property and human safety. While in towns and villages, they enter yards and stand outside house doors seeking garbage and meat scraps. They prevent people from going outdoors and moving about in their yards and on the streets. Charles Feazel, in *White Bear,* comments on a bear in town: "[It was] pacing back and forth outside two doorways, waiting for the unwary human who might become dinner."

Polar bears break into buildings and residences, though normally not into an occupied house, and often destroy greenhouses, storehouses and sheds, and sometimes homes. They kill dogs and harass people. Besides aggressively seeking foods, the polar bears also behave in some ways similar to brown and black bears—chew on, bite into, rip, claw, dig, and simply damage things. They tear up snowmobiles, too. One polar bear pushed its head through an open kitchen window of a house and quickly "inhaled" a bag of flour.

Outwitting Polar Bears

The term "outwitting" might just be inappropriate in the world of the polar bear. There are many measures used to outwit, but most are very direct and aggressive actions designed to detect, deter, and avoid these persistent bears. "Avoidance" may be a more descriptive word for preventing conflicts with polar bears. Stephen Herrero used the term in the subtitle of his extremely valuable book *Bear Attacks: Their Causes and Avoidance.* James Gary Shelton, in *Bear Encounter Survival Guide,* notes, "The first line of defense against bears is avoidance."

Historically, preventing conflicts in residential situations in polar bear country was very reactive. During the past ten to fifteen years or so, a proactive approach has become prevalent as residents have become more aware of how to prevent conflicts. They have an enhanced appreciation of the bears for their value as wild animals and an economic benefit for some communities.

Preventing Conflicts

The deterrents utilized in the Arctic with polar bears are basically the same as those used with brown and black bears elsewhere in North America. Most were developed by polar-bear biologists and managers in Canada.

Personal Actions to Avoid Conflicts

Properly handle food, garbage, and petroleum products.
Maintain good sanitation at the residence and workplace.
Avoid having hunting residue, blubber, and meat around residences.
Remove garbage daily.
Dry and smoke meat and fish inland.
Do not feed bears.

Remain away from areas where bears might be, such as whale gut piles.

Read posters and literature.

Talk with agency personnel, and seek bear information.

Obtain current bear reports from agency offices, and avoid areas of potential bear activity.

Listen to and heed radio reports of bear locations.

Report all bears.

Travel from houses in pairs.

Use vehicles instead of walking when bears might be in the area.

Keep vehicles away from residences.

Remain alert and vigilant.

Turn on lights before stepping outside during darkness.

Carefully look before stepping outside a building.

Educate children about bears.

Do not allow children to play outside during dark periods.

Children should never play outside unattended, and should play only in safe areas.

School children should be picked up and dropped off at their homes by buses.

Use vehicles (cars and snowmobiles) for protection and to chase off bears.

Use cracker shells to scare off bears.

Use dogs to detect and deter bears, and to warn people.

Use warning shots fired from shotguns or rifles to deter bears.

Use air horns to deter bears.

Use vehicle horns to chase bears.

Use thunderflashes (large firecrackers).

Use flare guns (projectile explodes loudly with bright flash).

Use propane cannons to deter bears.

Structural Measures to Avoid Conflicts

Houses in many areas are on pilings, with windows too high for entry.

Building doors are reinforced.

Bars are used to block doors from the inside.

Windows have bars (cage type) or are boarded up.

Fencing is utilized to enclose many buildings and areas (six-foot-high woven-wire and electric fences).

Iron cages are used for storage.

Metal buildings.

Snow is removed from around houses to increase visibility, and to keep bears from reaching windows.

Visibility is increased around houses, and hiding places for bears are reduced.

Agencies' Measures to Prevent Conflicts

Conduct street patrols to detect bears and warn people.

Main intensive patrol on Halloween.

Use spotlights during winter patrols.

Use vehicles to chase off bears.

Dumps are fenced and electrified.

Provide printed construction guidelines.

Provide bear-alert radio messages with bear locations.

Collect, haul, dump, and burn garbage daily.

Install electric fences around buildings and dumps.

Use aversive conditioning: rubber bullets, slugs, and other projectiles (plastic slugs have been ineffective).

Capture and remove bears from conflict areas.

Detection

The basic detection systems used by residents around their homes and yards are personal observation and barking dogs. More technical systems are used in and around Arctic settlements, villages, towns, research camps, and agency facilities to detect polar bears' approach and arrival. These include:

Trip-wire: A simple system whereby when a low-mounted wire is tripped over and pulled, breaking an electric circuit and triggering an audible alarm.

Microwave motion sensor: A large, elaborate system that creates microwaves between a transmitter and a receiver. When a bear passes through the beam, it interrupts the transmission, triggering an alarm.

Dogs: One or several dogs, trained to bark when a bear approaches, and tethered outside to warn of a bear's presence.

Infrared: Video recordings taken with infrared camcorders indicate a polar bear's presence on a display monitor.

Conventional Security Systems: Any system normally used for the protection of people and property, such as motion or sound detection.

Bear Monitors: People in and around developments, using spotlights, search for bears in order to warn residents of their approach and presence.

Preventing Polar Bear Attacks

People are threatened by polar bears, but rarely attacked, and injuries and deaths have become infrequent. Predation of humans is very rare. But the fear of attack is very common.

Churchill, Manitoba, Canada, a seaport on the west shore of Hudson Bay, is the home each October and November of the largest gathering of polar bears on earth, and is considered the "polar bear capital of the world." Approximately 1,200 bears gather here as they await the development of sea ice along Hudson Bay. Their presence attracts 12,000 to 15,000 tourists during this two-month period, a major boon to the economy of town.

Churchill is in the bears' territory, and they occasionally saunter through town. They are normally quite hungry and in an angry mood because they have eaten very little, living off fat reserves, for five to six months. The town has a safety program, Polar Bear Alert, which is managed by the Manitoba Department of Natural Resources, with objectives to protect people and property, and to protect bears from harassment and death. The program begins with education. It teaches people how to avoid confrontations (no feeding or harassing of bears), how to have minimum impact on bears, and how to react to a confrontation and an attack. While public education is paramount, the program contains some very direct and aggressive actions—detecting, monitoring, scaring away, capturing, removing from the area, and killing if necessary.

The Department of Natural Resources, along with cooperating agencies and institutions, aggressively keeps bears out of town and prevents conflicts by means of detection, close observations, street patrols, delineation (keeping bears and people separated), and "perimeter" trapping, with measures carried out twenty-four hours a day. If the bears are persistent, they are captured and placed in the Polar Bear Jail, and held until the ice returns. The jail is a building with large stalls, where the bears have minimal human contact. They receive no food, only water, so that they may continue their natural cycle.

Many of the measures applied in Churchill are found in other areas of the Arctic. Alaska's North Slope Borough has a very active polar-bear patrol and deterrence program.

Seven

Some Reminders

Bears represent something special—an element of wildness—that makes living with them mysterious, challenging, and exciting. Many residents of bear country claim that coexisting with bears is the lure for living there.

This close association with bears elevates our living experience to a higher level. We are displaying the ability to use our intelligence, to be flexible and adaptable, and to hold a sensitivity for an incredible species of wildlife. I hope people are able to live with bears forever, enjoying them as wild animals and an important ingredient of our lives. E.J. Fleming, in Adolph Murie's *The Grizzlies of Mount McKinley,* says, "It would be fitting, I think, if among the last man-made tracks on earth could be found the huge footprints of the great brown bear."

We are challenged to be creative, and to address the social situations that are necessary to have bears as neighbors. We must be willing to alter our lifestyles, to make the effort to outwit bears if we are to live in their country.

From these chapters, I hope you have gained the knowledge to prevent conflicts with bears, along with an understanding and appreciation of these marvelous animals. However, as you well know, our world is imperfect—living in bear country has risks. There are no guarantees of the success of our measures to outwit bears—they work extremely well, but there are always exceptions. Conflicts between humans and bears will always occur, as will strife among people. But conflicts must be minimized. People sometimes lose, but the bears always lose—maybe not directly, but when public sentiment turns against bears after a conflict occurs.

I have attempted to reach the lifestyles of many people, addressing their needs and methods to outwit bears. No two living situations are the same, and the approach on these pages is broad, but with measures that are specific. Most of you who read this book live in individual residences, where the vast majority of conflicts are normally associated with one or more of three attractants. When you protect your bird feeders, handle dog food appropriately, and keep your garbage secure, you will have met most of the challenge—at least 90 percent. You are almost there!

"I will soon be off again. . . . The mountains are calling and I must go. . . ."
                                        —John Muir

Appendix

Recommended Reading

My recommended reading list contains not only writings that apply directly to outwitting bears, but also includes books that provide general bear knowledge and bear stories, fact and fable, that are just plain interesting and enjoyable reading. Read, study, and learn more about bears, especially if they are your neighbors.

Adler, Bill, Jr. *Outwitting Critters*. New York: Lyons & Burford, Publishers, 1992.

———. *Outwitting Squirrels*. Chicago: Chicago Review, 1996.

———. *Outwitting Deer*. New York: The Lyons Press, 1999.

Brown, Gary. *The Great Bear Almanac*. New York: Lyons and Burford, Publishers, 1993.

———. *Safe Travel In Bear Country*. New York: Lyons and Burford, Publishers, 1996.

Brown, David E., and John Murray. *The Last Grizzly*. Tucson: The University of Arizona Press, 1988.

Cardoza, James E. *The Black Bear in Massachusetts*. Westborough: Massachusetts Division of Fisheries & Wildlife, 1976.

Cramond, Mike. *Killer Bears*. New York: Outdoor Life Books/Charles Scribner's Sons, 1981.

———. *Of Bears and Man*. Norman, OK: University of Oklahoma Press, 1986.

Domico, Terry, and Mark Newman. *Bears of the World*. New York: Facts on File, 1988.

Dufresne, Frank. *No Room For Bears*. New York: Holt, Rinehart and Winston, Inc., 1965.

Feazel, Charles T. *White Bear*. New York: Henry Holt and Company, 1990.

Gowans, Fred R. *Mountain Man & Grizzly*. Orem, Utah: Mountain Grizzly Publications, 1986.

Halfpenny, James. *A Field Guide to Mammal Tracking in Western America*. Boulder, CO: Johnson Publishing Company, 1986.

Haynes, Bessie D., and Edgar Haynes. *The Grizzly Bear*. Norman: University of Oklahoma Press, 1966.

Herrero, Stephen. *Bear Attacks: Their Causes and Avoidance*. New York: Nick Lyons Books/Winchester Press, 1985.

Hygnstrom, Scott E., Robert M. Timm, Gary E. Larson. *Prevention and Control of Wildlife Damage*. Lincoln, NE: University of Nebraska, 1994.

Kaniut, Larry. *Alaska Bear Tales*. Anchorage: Alaska Northwest Publishing Co., 1983.

———. *More Alaska Bear Tales*. Anchorage: Alaska Northwest Books, 1989.

Kipling, Rudyard. *The Jungle Book*. H. Wolff, 1895 (Doubleday & Co., New York, 1948).

Koch, Thomas J. *The Year of the Polar Bear*. New York: The Bobbs-Merrill Company, Inc., 1975.

Kurten, Bjorn. *The Cave Bear Story*. New York: Columbia University Press, 1995.

Laycock, George. *The Wild Bears*. New York: Outdoor Life Books, 1986.

Leopold, Aldo. *A Sand County Almanac*. New York: Oxford University Press, Inc., 1949.

McCracken, Harold. *The Beast that Walks Like Man*. Garden City, New York: The Garden City Press, 1955.

McMillion, Scott. *Mark of the Grizzly*. Helena, MT: Falcon Press, 1998.

McNamee, Thomas. *The Grizzly Bear*. New York: Alfred A. Knopf, 1984.

Murie, Adolph. *The Grizzlies of Mount McKinley*. Washington, D.C.: United States Department of the Interior, 1981.

Orwell, George. *Animal Farm*. New York: Harcourt, Brace and Company, 1946.

Osteen, Phyllis. *Bears Around the World*. New York: Coward-McCann, 1966.

Ovsyanikov, Nikita. *Polar Bears: Living With The White Bear*. Stillwater, MN: Voyageur Press, Inc., 1996.

Rockwell, David. *Giving Voice to Bear*. Niwot, CO: Roberts Rinehart Publishers, 1991.

Schullery, Paul. *American Bears: Selections from the Writings of Theodore Roosevelt*. Boulder: Colorado Associated University Press, 1983.

———. *The Bears of Yellowstone*. Niwot: Roberts Rinehart, Inc., 1986.

———. *The Bear Hunter's Century*. New York: Dodd, Mead & Co., 1988.

———. *Pregnant Bears & Crawdad Eyes*. Seattle: The Mountaineers, 1991.

Service, Robert. *The Spell of the Yukon*. New York: Dodd, Mead & Company, 1907.

Shelton, James Gary. *Bear Encounter Survival Guide*. Hagensborg, B.C., Canada: Pogany Productions, 1994.

———. *Bear Attacks: The Deadly Truth*. Hagensborg, B.C., Canada: Shelton Productions, 1998.

Shepard, Paul, and Barry Sanders. *The Sacred Paw*. New York: Viking Penguin, Inc., 1985.

Storer, Tracy I., and Lloyd P. Tevis, Jr. *California Grizzly*. Berkeley: University of California Press, 1955.

There is an assortment of bulletins and brochures with valuable information related to living and traveling in bear country. Distributed by wildlife-management agencies of the federal, state, provincial, territorial, county, borough, and district governments, and private organizations across the continent, they are well worth obtaining and studying.

Index